DEFYING THE FATES:

THE REMARKABLE STORY OF A JEW WHO SURVIVED IN NAZI EUROPE

By Henry H. Gleisner

Center for Holocaust and Humanity Education
HUC - JIR - Cincinnati

*To Mr Weinman
with best wishes
Henry H. [signature]*

PUBLISHED BY:
ALPINE I
P.O. Box 542
Oxford, MI 48371 U.S.A.
COPYRIGHT 2000
ALL RIGHTS RESERVED

**COPYRIGHT© APPLIED 2000 BY
HENRY H. GLEISNER
LIBRARY OF CONGRESS
CONTROL NUMBER 00-091099**

ISBN #   0-9704 203-0-7

DEFYING THE FATES

The Remarkable Story of a Jew Who Survived in Nazi Europe

This autobiography is more than a powerful memoir. It is extraordinary. There are many Holocaust survivor stories. There are many eyewitness accounts of the Nazi horror. But none that I have read bears this unique combination of pathos, ingenuity and defiance.

When I first heard the personal saga of Henry Gleisner, I encouraged him to record it. This story of a young Jewish man who managed to elude Nazi detection at the center of the German world challenges the odds that the fates normally provide. Austria, Poland, Ukraine, Crimea, Italy and Germany are all settings in this amazing tale. Henry's pluck, courage, and compassion manifest themselves, whether he is dealing with sadists, bureaucrats, partisans, friends or family. Others, in the same circumstances might not have survived.

This memoir provides many important political insights. The knowledge of the Holocaust was widespread in the German world almost from the very beginning. The German army and its officer leaders were accomplices with the murder squads in the destruction of Polish and Russian Jewry. The racist humiliation of the Poles and Ukrainians deprived the Germans of potential allies. The Nazis, despite all their reported fanatic idealism, were hopelessly corrupt. And the refusal of postwar German bureaucrats to acknowledge that a Jew could survive the surveillance of the Nazis is a tribute to a persistent German arrogance and stupidity.

I could not put down this memoir once I began to read it. This story of danger, horror and adventure is compelling.

Sherwin T. Wine
Rabbi, The Birmingham Temple

DEDICATION

Surviving Holocaust victims display an astounding accuracy of memory. Having met and talked with many of them, I have found this capacity quite amazing. I myself can recall minute details. This does not include the accurate historical sequence of events.

There was and still is an overwhelming reluctance to recall, relive, write down, or even discuss the horrors of the Holocaust. I have found it extremely painful and I had to overcome a strong psychological reluctance to write down what I saw and did.

My overwhelming thanks go above all to my wife, Nancy Jo, who encouraged me, helped me, and worked hard on my manuscript.

My dear friend, Rabbi Sherwin Wine, reminded me and prodded me throughout the years to do what he thought was important for me and for others.

My second cousin, Krzysztof Prochaska, helped me, not only with advice, but also by sending old family photos, maps, and documentary background materials from Poland.

Thank you!

Oxford, Michigan
July 2000

WITH MY MOTHER – VIENNA 1928

WITH MY FATHER – VIENNA 1932

**UNCLE LEOPOLD GLEISNER
AUSTRIAN ARMY - 1914**

**GRANDFATHER GLEISNER
KRAKOW 1895**

THIS IS WHO I AM

I was born in Vienna, Austria and attended schools there until my father became CEO of a motion picture company in Warsaw, Poland. My family moved there in 1936, before World War II began.

Because of my family's activities in the film industry, my father was on the German Gestapo (Geheime Staats Polizei --the Nazi State Secret Police) list of enemies. Upon the outbreak of WW II in September 1939, and with the advance of the German armies into western Poland, my family fled to eastern Poland, which in turn was invaded and occupied by the Soviets. There I continued in school and acquired additional language skills (Russian, Polish, Ukrainian, French, English, etc.)

In 1940 When Germany invaded the Soviet Union, we came immediately under German occupation. My parents, as well as many other family members, perished in concentration camps. I was able to escape with false documents, working and traveling in various parts of Europe, winding up in 1944 in Italy, and at War's end in 1945 in Austria. In northern Italy I was active with the Italian underground, joined the Allied Forces, and eventually worked with American Military Government in Austria.

After a stint with UNRRA (United Nations Relief and Rehabilitation Agency) in refugee camps, I entered the U. S., becoming a U. S. Citizen in 1952.

I founded and headed St. Lawrence Sales, an import and export company of sports and recreational equipment, for 35 years. We received the coveted "E" Award" for "Excellence in Exporting: from President Bush in 1989. The award was presented in Lake Orion, Michigan by then Congressman Broomfield.

****

CHAPTER 1

LIFE IN VIENNA

For a period during World War I, my father went to officer's candidate school in Muerzzuschlag, Styria. He was very lucky and was never sent to the front, for before his training was completed, the War ended.

After they were married, my parents went on various vacations about which they told me. One vacation they spent on the northern island of Ruegen in the North Sea. They must have been fortunate that summer, for this island is normally known to have very cold weather, even during July and August. Another vacation was in Fulpness in the Tyrolean Alps.

My father's family was of very solid Jewish background, and my grandparents and great-grandparents were observant Jews. I met my grandmother once in Krakow when she was a very old lady. Oddly enough, my grandfathers on both sides were paper merchants. My parents were non-observant Jews, and although a Synagogue was very near where we lived, we seldom attended. To reach it we had to go through a passageway of an apartment building, which ended in a tiny backyard square. There stood the ornate, large Muellergasse Synagogue.

During the High Holidays my father would sometimes take me to a service. Neither my mother nor my grandmother ever accompanied us. In retrospect, I think I know the reason. This was a Conservative Synagogue where the women were seated separately on a balcony. I am sure that neither my mother, nor my grandmother looked favorably on such an arrangement. They were emancipated, well-educated women who spoke their minds without hesitation.

I had a very close and loving relationship with my grandmother. In spite of the inbred anti-Semitism in Vienna, she admired the elderly Emperor and the old Empire greatly. She said to me on one occasion, "I am sorry that you are born too late. You will never see and witness the grandeur of Vienna as the capital of a Great Empire!" Her Jewishness was beyond question. She even told me the story of Theodor Herzl, and explained the Zionist ideals and politics. There was no doubt that she was very sympathetic toward Zionism.

These were strange times, inasmuch as a little boy about ten years of age would be taught and given explanations of a complicated political nature. But all of Europe was highly politicized in those times and politics were passionately and sometimes aggressively discussed among us students in school.

The school curriculum included a weekly lesson in "religion." The classes divided into three groups: the Catholics, the Protestants, and the Jews. My group of approximately 20 Jewish students was taught by a highly progressive, strongly Zionist Rabbi, by the name of Bronner. Professor Bronner indoctrinated all of us with the Zionist viewpoint. One of his remarks remains vividly in memory. "Go to Palestine. There is no future for you boys in Europe!" We did not comprehend what he meant. But many years later, I thought about his message, and admired the foresight of this great man.

Vienna was very much an intellectual center with an extremely progressive, assimilated Jewish community. In the 2nd District there were many Orthodox Jews, but the major part of the Jewish community in Vienna was either reform, totally non-practicing or agnostic. They influenced the cultural and artistic life of Vienna in the milieu of theater, music, poetry, painting, journalism, and literature -- all the arts.

My mother's family came from Hungary. My grandmother's and my grandfather's families were all from Budapest and Temesvar (Timisoara). My grandmother spoke little Hungarian, because she lived all her life in Vienna. Part of her family came from Timisoara, which once belonged to Hungary but is now part of Romania. Grandmother was a fierce Austro-Hungarian nationalist and Monarchist. She was very upset after World War I when this part of Hungary was given to Romania. She always said, "They tore the heart out of Hungary!," which, of course, was a great exaggeration, as well as somewhat off course geographically.

During the summer of 1933 a cousin invited my mother and me to Temesvar (Timisoara) in Rumania. Her name was Margit Eisner, and she had a son about my age. My mother packed up our things and on we went by railway to Timisoara. On the Hungarian border there was a serious incident. When the Hungarian immigration officials found that I did not have a transit visa to Romania, they wanted to send my mother back to Vienna with me. After long discussions, one of the commanding officers became restive about the train being held up over this stupidity. Finally my mother persuaded them to allow us to go on.

A huge automobile (a Buick, no less) picked us up from the station. For the times this was an unusual and luxurious mode of transportation. The Eisner family owned large tracts of forests in the area, had a big sawmill and sold lumber. It was a wonderful vacation because my cousin Franz and I roamed freely around the whole area. Luckily, our parents never discovered what we were up to. A narrow gage railroad with heavy little cars to carry the wood ran on their property, and we found it a wonderful playground. It was great fun to ride the cars down the hills, jumping off at the last moment before they crashed into a barrier -- a very dangerous activity.

Another bit of excitement occurred when one of the mechanical saws -- a big machine with about twelve blades -- was sawing through a huge tree trunk. It hit upon a World War I grenade that lodged inside that tree. There was a tremendous explosion that blew out half of the installation and injured several of the workers. It was a terrible accident.

The conditions in Romania were appalling. The poverty was so intense that most of the peasants were barefoot, and the agricultural goods were so cheap that it was hard to believe. I was sent to the market with my cousin to buy some melons. We bought two and paid 50 Banis, which was one half a Lei -- a fraction of a penny. The peasant woman gave us another melon as a gift because she felt that she had overcharged us by taking this almost meaningless amount of money.

After this summer vacation, we kept in touch with the Eisner family by mail until the outbreak of the War. I have never heard from this branch of my family ever again.

My mother's family, though Jewish, was not observant. Once a year during Christmas time we made a visit to my Uncle Zhiga and his wife, Aunt Helene. Uncle Zhiga was a retired Colonel of the old Austrian Koeniglich & Kaiserliche (Royal and Imperial) Army. He served in a court-guard regiment in Vienna, and they were "very distinguished people." Interestingly enough, they spoke German with a heavy Hungarian accent. Among themselves they spoke exclusively Hungarian. This was typical of the multi-national character of the former Austro-Hungarian Empire. It really was a precursor of a form of "United Nations." Austria was governed by the aristocrats of all its member nations. The palaces of the princes, dukes, counts, and barons carrying Polish, Czech, Croatian, and Hungarian names bear witness to this patrimony in Vienna until today. Unfortunately, this system fell apart for several reasons: The rise of strident nationalism, the sufferings and disruption of World War I, and the inept and bureaucratic way the Viennese central government functioned.

  As a little boy of about 8, I was dressed and coifed to the utmost when we made our visit to Aunt Helene and Uncle Zhiga. They lived in an apartment on the Wiedner Hauptstrasse, a very elegant district. I was taught a few words of Hungarian. I had to say, "Jo napot Zsiga bacsi" "Hello, Uncle Zsiga;" "Kezet Csokolom," "I kiss your hand, Madame." I had to stand very straight with my fingers to the side seams of my pants, and I was drilled like for no other occasion. Even my father joined the effort to make me "presentable." He was not usually very "disciplinary" and certainly not keen on military things and doings. But...when we went to wish "Merry Christmas and a Happy New Year" to Onkel Zhiga and Tante Helene, I was put into a sailor uniform and told repeatedly not to speak up except when spoken to.

My grandma, who was the closest relative to Onkel Zhiga, never joined us. Upon reflection, I suspect it was because they adopted the Catholic faith. How else, I wonder, could he have become a Colonel in an Imperial Regiment?

After dinner I was told that I could go and play in Uncle Zhiga's study where there was all kinds of paraphernalia of the old Colonel. I attacked Turkish invaders with his saber, and on one occasion I tried on his stiff leather puttees (these were like boots without the foot part). Since they came up way above my knees, I clomped around like on stilts -- like the Tin Man in "The Wizard of Oz." My uncle and my father came into the room to check on the thumping. Uncle Zhiga laughed heartily at my awkward marching and decided to make a gift of those wonderful leather puttees to me. He insisted, though my parents were rather embarrassed to accept. I felt those puttees were very special and enjoyed strutting around in them as much as Uncle Zhiga seemed to enjoy giving them to me. They were items that to me had a good deal of historical and sentimental significance. To have an Uncle at the Court of the old Kaiser Franz Josef was something of which I felt very proud. The old gentleman seemed to sense this. Whatever became of those puttees???

The period around the time I was born saw great hyperinflation throughout Germany and Austria. My daughter gave me a newspaper printed on my birth date that showed that French Franc advanced very strongly on the week previous to my birth. This was during the period of the Weimar Republic in Germany. One U. S. Dollar was worth first thousands, then a million, and finally billions of Reichsmarks.

These were followed by some of the golden years prior to the economic upheavals of the depression

I had a very good and joyful time as a child. My grandmother usually took care of me because my parents were often socially occupied, going to the theater, movies, art exhibits, receptions, dining with friends. Once a week they had a bridge club get-together at the Kaffeehaus Landsmann on the Schottenring.

Although I was very close to both my parents, I was closest to my grandmother. She was the source of a great amount of education and tried to instill in me a hunger for knowledge, particularly in geography and history. She constantly told me stories about all kinds of things that she had read in the various magazines and newspapers, and she also took me to the movies every week, a great shared pleasure.

As I grew older I was often sent on my own to fetch groceries, and sometimes I went to the pub around the corner and carried back a foaming pitcher of beer. The pub was a stand-up bar located next door to the police station. All the local police used to drink there at all times of the day or night.

Our apartment house did not have an elevator -- we had to walk up and down four stories, and for old grandmother that became increasingly difficult. I remember grandmother and our maid carrying up buckets full of coal from the basement to heat our apartment.

One summer we had a visitor -- my cousin Sandor from Budapest. He was a young doctor, just graduated, and in practice at one of the Vienna hospitals. He was a very nice young man and I was greatly interested in him, though he did not have much time for a small worshipful boy. One day, perhaps two months after he came to live with us, he suddenly disappeared. I found out afterwards that he was a morphine addict and had stolen morphine from the hospital. When his theft was discovered, he went to sit down on a bench in the Stadtpark, where he shot himself in the head. These things I found out much later, for at the time I was a small child, and my parents did not want me to know of such things.

In the late fall, my grandmother succumbed to an illness and died. This was a great loss and shock to me. My grandmother was so close to me, took care of me, devoted a great amount of time to my education, and taught me many things -- more so actually than my mother.

We employed a maid, Mitzi, from a peasant family in the Burgenland, an agricultural district that is close to the Hungarian border. Because of my sadness and my difficulty in accepting the loss of my grandma, the maid arranged to take me along with her on her Christmas vacation to her home farm. My parents thought it was a good idea to get me away from my apartment and from Vienna into an environment that was totally strange to me. We went by post bus to the Burgenland, and were picked up from the postal station by a horse drawn wagon.

The farm was small, and by today's standards very backward. Mitzi's family still worked the fields with the horses, and did not have any tractors or mechanical devices.

The farm itself consisted of several buildings. The main building where they lived had a thatched roof in the old fashioned way. The walls were whitewashed and there were wooden floors, an outhouse, and a cow barn bigger than the house.

It was an interesting and new experience for a child of 11 years. They treated me with a sense of amusement because I was so citified and also strange to them. But I learned a lot about the upkeep and work on a farm and the maintenance of the animals. They had dogs, cats, cattle, and sheep, which had to be fed and cared for, and I tried to help along.

Shortly before Christmas the big event was the slaughter of a very large pig. I was assigned to hold on to the little curly tail of the pig while they slaughtered it. The sectioning of the pig and the making of the smoked meat, sausage, and all the other activities connected with the pig slaughter was a revelation to me. Virtually every part of the pig was used in one way or another. Even the guts of the pig had to be washed out and cleaned to be used for sausage skins, which were filled with cooked, mashed meat. This unusual Christmas vacation at Mitzi's farm lasted two weeks and opened up another view of life that I had never seen before.

On Sundays in Vienna, my parents, and often times my father alone, took me out in Vienna to various places. Once we went to the Urania, which was an astronomy museum. One Sunday we went to the Museum of Art or Natural History. On summer weekends we went swimming in the Danube or to a pool in the Prater, which was the big Viennese amusement park.

My mother was very sports oriented. One summer week-end we all three went to the Doebling Strandbad, which was a city-owned public swimming pool and recreation area where we paid a small entrance fee. My mother participated vigorously in gymnastics exercises, in the process of which she tore a tendon in her knee, and they had to transport her by ambulance to a hospital where they slapped on a cast for the full length of her leg. She had the cast for 6 or 7 weeks, and we all commiserated with her and helped her along. It wasn't very long after the cast came off that she started out again with the exercises, first slowly, and then more vigorously until she got back into shape. She held an enthusiastic attitude about athletics, and encouraged me to take up skiing. Arriving in the U. S. A. after the War, I used my extensive knowledge and capability in this sport helped me to become one of the first ski instructors in Michigan.

I took up swimming, probably under the influence of my mother, who was a competitive swimmer in her younger years. She belonged to swim clubs and competed in swimming meets. She entered me in a swim club and in wintertime I would go once a week to the Diana Bad to swim under the direction of an instructor. The Diana Bad was an indoor swimming complex with two Olympic sized pools, health facilities and large dressing rooms. One of the pools had artificial waves every 5 minutes. We were trained in the other 50-meter swimming pool.

Before belonging to swimming clubs, however, I had to learn to swim. My parents spent a lot of money and time to give me swimming lessons. We spent one summer in Bad Ischl. There some dim-witted instructor strapped me into a wide band and held me above the water like on a fishing pole while I made swimming motions. I never got deeper into the water, nor did I learn to swim from him, of course.

In those days a wooden swimming pool of Kaiser Franz Josef's time still existed in Bad Ischl. It was called the Damen Bad for it was a ladies only facility, though of course, the ladies were allowed to bring small children along. Thus I saw and bathed in the wooden swimming pool of Empress Elisabeth (Sissy). It was later used by

Baroness Schratt, an opera singer, and Franz Josef's mistress, for whom he also built a villa.

{It is perhaps curious that shortly after the War I again found myself in Bad Ischl. After the Americans had marched in, I went to the office of the Mayor, turned in my false papers on which I had survived the War, and obtained my regular birth certificate and other papers through the police center in Vienna. I was also assigned an apartment. Lo and behold, that apartment was one of the floors in the old Schratt Villa.}

After many other attempts to teach me to swim, I was sent to a children's camp one summer for a two-week vacation. On this occasion, one of the other kids gave me a good push, and I fell into the swimming pool and started to swim on my own. Thus I finally learned how! This experience perhaps shaped my opinion that the best way to learn something is through actually being forced to do it.

Vienna was an exciting city in the 1930's. Kuba (my father, Jacob's nickname) was a gentle man. He worked for many years as a medium level executive at the Wiener Bankverein. He was an assistant to the then powerful and flamboyant Director Kiesler. Among his hobbies, the Herr Director was a competitive rower at one of the top, exclusive rowing clubs on the Danube. This activity most probably cost him his life, since he succumbed to a heart attack while rowing. This occurred just at the onset of the impact of the Great Depression. His beautiful and talented daughter, at the age of 17 made the notorious movie "Extase" in which she appeared stark naked. It was the first time for such an exhibition in a commercial film. Soon she moved to Hollywood and became the world-famous Hedy Lamarr. She was my first crush!

Not only was Hedy a gifted actress, but she was also very accomplished in other areas. She held a patent on a broad-band protection device that prevented enemy radio from diverting programmed mines launched by submarines or warships, of enormous aid to the U. S. Navy during World War II. She died in February 2000 in Orlando, Florida at the age of 86.

The death of Director Kiesler was seriously detrimental to my father. He lost his foremost and probably only "benefactor" in the bank. The personnel relations were insidious, political, and vicious. Soon my father was terminated with a small payment and pension.

This pension payment disappeared without a trace after the Austrian Anschluss. My inquiries with the successor bank, the Creditanstalt, right after the War and until now have met with polite letters to me stating that, "All records have been destroyed, and they can not find any trace of such an account."

My father had worked for them for over fifteen years. No reasonable chance existed for a banker, 44 years old, Jewish, without access to sizable capital to find employment in 1935 during the Depression.

Thereupon, my family moved to Warsaw, Poland, in 1936, where my father's family owned a very successful film distribution and production business called "MUZA-FILM."

I had to adjust myself to the new environment and learn Polish on very short notice. In addition to attending school classes, I had, two private tutors on a daily basis seven days a week. I also attended English classes in the evening at the British Consulate, and had French lessons once a week in the evening.

In 1939 a few days after the outbreak of the War, my family departed Warsaw fleeing the bombardment and the advancing German armies to the city of Lwow, an eastern Polish city. There we were overrun by the Soviets, who occupied the eastern part of Poland (the infamous Ribbentrop-Molotov Pact.)

I went to school for a year in the Soviet Union, learning Russian, another language. Today I speak seven languages fluently, The Germans attacked again a year later and the Soviets were overrun. Lwow was occupied within two days.

After that, very hard times came upon my family. We had to move several times, until we were confined in the soon to be exterminated Lwow Ghetto. A Vienna born Jew who was brought up in Austria and Poland, I escaped from the ghetto in Lwow in 1941 while still a teen-ager. I was 16 years old. I had to conceal my Jewish background in order to provide for my family and help them survive.

Trying to save my parents, I repeatedly sneaked into an outpost of the Janowska concentration camp near Lwow to bring my father some food. Despite these efforts, both my parents perished in the camps.

Disguised as a Pole by the name of Tadeusz Chwistek, I worked in various places, among others, in the kitchen of the headquarters of the Italian Expeditionary Force. Clad first in the black slave labor uniform of Polish forced labor, I worked my way up slowly by transferring from one firm to another, By play-acting (I pretended to gradually "learn" German, which really was my mother tongue), and building up my file of German documents, I finally became a warehouse foreman for a German building firm of Dr.-Ingineur Wilhelm Stickel, a road and bridge construction firm working on contract for the

German Army/Air Force. I stealthily continued this transformation until the Germans began to assume I was one of them.

Later in the beige uniform of the Organisation Todt, I traveled on company business all over the Nazi occupied Soviet Union and Western Europe, even paying a visit to the company's headquarters in Berlin.

This firm transferred me from one building site to another: to the Ukraine, the Crimea, to Berlin, Krakow, and then to northern Italy, and finally back to Austria. In the process of all these transfers, I was able to travel on legitimate and illegitimate travel papers throughout Europe, including Vienna, Prague, Warsaw, Krakow, Kiev, Berlin, Frankfurt, Munich, Udine, Milano, and other cities.

During my work on military airport runways, I was able to join the Italian underground resistance movement, and sabotaged the very same construction at night that I helped to build during daytime hours.

Toward the end of the War, one of the directors of the building firm built himself a small house in the mountains of Austria, and ordered me to help him with the task. Eventually, the American Army occupied that part of Austria and I then became active in the work of the American Military Government in this part of Austria.

Hidden in the uniform of a German road construction unit, I survived the Holocaust. Many years later the West German government refused to believe it was possible.

So perfect was this mask that after the war I had problems returning to my true identity. I eventually managed to convince the Austrian authorities to issue me new documents for emigration to the United States.

Many years later, the over-confident bureaucracy of the Federal Republic of Germany, who had no "direct remembrance" of the War years, rejected my claim that Henry Gleisner and Tadeusz Chwistek were one and the same person.

"There are serious doubts that you could change your name and have that accepted by German authorities considering that, at the time, an air-tight police registration system was in operation," the Federal Insurance Office for Employees (Bundesversicherungsanstalt Fuer Angestellte) wrote on July 3, 1984 in a decision to deny my claim for compensation. Yet sworn affidavits from witnesses and original documents in my possession confirmed my identity beyond a doubt.

I transformed myself into a Pole and then to an "almost German" because I resented the idea of becoming a passive victim of Auschwitz's gas chambers. The odds against my survival were tremendous, and I had many close calls with death, among others, interrogation by the dreaded German secret police, the Gestapo.

My lack of obvious Semitic features, my language skills, an excellent education, a keen understanding of the German character, ingenuity in dealing with the Nazi bureaucracy, strong nerves and determination all worked to my advantage. One might say that I won this intricate game for life within the Nazi system.

CHAPTER 2

SCHUBERT SCHULE AND WASA-GYMNASIUM

My elementary school was the Schubert Schule located right across the street from our apartment. I attended this school for 4 years.

It was a boys' school. A short distance down the street was the women's high school, which my mother had attended. She continued her friendship with some of her schoolmates for many years. Considering that she went to school during World War I, she belonged to a swim club, a hiking society, and a choir, and played tennis. She used to play the guitar and sing to it, especially during hiking excursions. Two of her best friends were Mrs. Singer and Mrs. Steiner. Both of them had sons of the same age as I. We attended the same classes, and became close friends of the second generation.

On my first day of school my father insisted on taking me to the school, which was only a few steps away from our house. He first took me to a nearby grocery store and bought me my little lunch, which I was supposed to eat during lunchtime intermission. He bought too much food for me, and I cried because I was afraid that they would press me to eat up everything that I brought along. He assured me that I could bring whatever I couldn't eat back home. It seems he was very proud to bring his six-year old son for the first day of school. I never went to kindergarten. I don't believe that in those days there was an early schooling offered, such as pre-school, or kindergarten.

My friend Rolf Steiner and I attended a ski camp conducted by his father, who was a renowned mountaineer and skier. Our ski camp took place at the Feuerkogel during winter vacation 1935.

About that time the Civil War broke out in Austria --the Reds vs. the Blacks. The overwhelming majority of the population of Vienna was Reds. Then came Social Democrats and a contingent of Communists. They were aligned against the Catholic Center Party, and the Austro-Fascists. All over the city Vienna were low rent social apartment houses for workers.

Both political parties had their own armies. When it came to a showdown, the Austrian military, under the command of a Colonel Fey brought artillery up onto the surrounding hills of the Vienna Woods and started to systematically bombard the apartment blocks of the workers. The Blacks won this confrontation, and within their grouping the Austro-Fascists took over the government under Chancellor Dollfuss. He was murdered later on in the Chancellery by a group of Nazis, who would not tolerate any other group. This new government affected even the school children. We had to wear "red-white-red" pins and our curriculum was changed greatly under the influence of the Catholic hierarchy. Even school children were highly politicized in those times. My father, who sympathized strongly with the Reds, as an old line Social Democrat, took my mother and myself on a tour by taxicab to all the bombarded apartment complexes. This was a kind of political education for me.

The inhumanity and ferocity of the breaking up of the Social Democrat Militias and the bombardment of apartment houses, killing and maiming women and children, was a foreshadowing of the atrocities of World War II, which was to begin a few years later.

However, in 1936 my father took on a new job in Warsaw Poland, and he, my mother, and I moved there. We sold all our furniture and we spent the last couple of days in the Hotel France on the Ringstrasse in Vienna before boarding our train at the Ostbahnhof toward a new country and new experiences.

For a young boy of 12 years old, this was a great adventure, and although my mother cried and was very unhappy to leave her beloved Vienna, I felt that to meet new people, learn new languages, and to have access to interesting new ways of living was exciting, and I was happy about it. Part of my feelings was caused also by the increasing anti-Semitism that I encountered in the gymnasium (high school). The constant battle between the Nationalists and Pro-Nazi pupils against the more liberal and Jewish students was not a very pleasant milieu.

In the early 30's I started going to an Austrian government "Gymnasium," the famous "WASA-Gymnasium in Vienna. The government gymnasiums were of the highest standards and tuition free. They used a "sieving system" -- in the first grade we had a total of about ninety children in two separate classrooms. In the 8th grade (Octa) the graduating class consisted of eight young men. This system, as in the Ecole Superieur in France, guaranteed the graduate's entry into the university and fast advancing government positions if the graduate so desired.

All our subjects were obligatory and failure in a single one caused expulsion. In languages we studied: Latin, two semesters of Ancient Greek, English, French, German (language and literature). Under mathematics were geometry, trigonometry, and calculus. We also learned chemistry, both organic and non-organic, physics, geography and economic geography, history -- Austrian and world history, botany and zoology, and on and on.

Naturally, the subjects were distributed over various years and semesters.

The alternatives were for a youngster to enter a trade school, or to study in a private school. The private schools were expensive, and for the most part scholastically undesirable. Compare this with today's controversies about our public school systems: charter schools, vouchers, public vs. private schools, etc.

The year of my entry there were so many qualified applicants that the so-called "Prima" (first grade) was divided into One-A and One-B. The education minister (an Austro-Fascist) decided that the approximately 50 pupils of One-A were the Catholics, and the remaining 40 (predominantly Jewish, but also Protestants and non-affiliated) were put into One-B. This system was so bad that it was abolished after one year. It created animosities, name calling, pitched battles after school, and did not serve any positive purpose. Although we didn't have school uniforms, it was obligatory to wear a pin on our lapels showing the Red-White-Red colors of Austria with the inscription "Seid Einig" (Be United!). This was also the party pin of the Austro-Fascist political party of Chancellor Dollfuss. We were checked, and if we forgot our pin, we had to go home. Dividing the classes by religion did not contribute toward uniting all of Austria's citizens.

Although the Austro-Fascists ("The Fatherland Front") were similarly like the Nazis of the extreme right, the two movements hated each other and fought ferociously. The Dollfuss regime even created a concentration camp where they imprisoned leading Nazis. The conditions were very benign, however, and this camp cannot be compared in any way with the subsequent camps created by the Hitlerian criminals. Eventually the Chancellor of Austria, Mr. Englebert Dollfuss was murdered in his Vienna Chancellery on the Ballhausplatz by a gang of Nazi Brownshirts.

I remember in particular our gymnastics teacher, Dr. Stephan, a small man with a bitter face. He was an outspoken Nazi and he made life miserable for some of us in the class. For some minor infraction he put me into two gymnastic rings, which were then drawn up, and I was left to hang there in the air with the rings under my armpits for about five minutes. It was painful and created in me a tremendous amount of hatred and resistance against this bully. The combativeness of my make-up was developed all though these years, and it started right there at the Wasa Gymnasium in the gym class.

CHAPTER 3

OUT OF THE KITCHEN OF THE EMPIRE

    At our home in Michigan we have a lot of wild apple trees in our yard, I gather the good ones every year, and it has become a custom that we always make a whole bunch of apple strudels in October. A couple of years ago when my good wife made up a bunch of 20 or so strudels, which we eat, freeze, and share with our friends who admire them, I made the foolish remark that "this apple strudel isn't quite the way my grandmother used to make it." I felt that the lack of "semmel broesel" (bread crumbs) made the strudel non-authentic. Real Viennese apple strudel, I explained, must have breadcrumbs and raisins and should not have nuts. For reasons that escape me, my wife became quite furious, and told me that from now on if I wanted "AUTHENTIC VIENNESE APFEL STRUDEL" I should make it myself!

    At that time I had a "flashback" to my early childhood, and I remembered the small kitchen in our large apartment on Gruene Torgasse 12, Wien IX, Alsergrund (my parents drilled me to remember my address and phone number, A18677, for emergencies, and I remember them still today). As a small boy, I sat near my grandmother on a little bench observing "Oma" as she slaved away on a big table that was covered with a thick tablecloth. On this she sprinkled flour and then stretched the dough with her fists slowly, slowly all around to make dough so thin and fine that one could read a newspaper through it. This is almost a lost art. (My wife's own grandmother – who was also born in pre-war Austro-Hungary -- declared that Nancy was stupid and inept because she made holes in the strudel dough when she tried to stretch it). My Oma admonished me very strongly not to move, and above all not to open any windows or doors because the draught would ruin the strudel dough.

Today when I make the strudel myself out of Filo dough, I can very well understand the reason. I have to cover the Filo dough with a wet towel in order to prevent it from drying out. I watched as Oma carefully added the sugar and raisins to the mashed apples along with all the other ingredients; and then came the rolling of the strudel by flipping the tablecloth, and the delicate placing of the roll on the baking pan without breaking it. Although I was probably only 6 years old, I had total recall.

When I was so savagely admonished by my wife, I decided that I would re-create the genuine, authentic, 100% Viennese Apfel Strudel all by myself. It was a lot of work, peeling the apples, preparing the stuffing, delicately rolling it into the dough, baking, etc. But even my wife had the grace to admit that it was truly the real, genuine item, and considerably better than hers. Since then I have become the official resident Apfel Strudel stuffer in our home, much to the amusement and enjoyment of friends and neighbors.

This brings to mind many other happy memories. My father used to take walks on Sunday mornings at all times of the year. He often took me along, and would point out some historical marker or place of significance and give me a little background of happenings in the past. This type of early education in my childhood provoked a life-long interest in history and geography. I wish that more children of our friends here in America had this interest and understanding of events and places in the past.

On cold Sunday mornings we would stop about 10:00 A.M. at the Brewery Grabner, which served a "Zehnerjause" (second breakfast or Ten O'clock Snack) of so-called "Fruehstuecks Goulash" or "Breakfast Goulash." This was a small plate of really good Goulash with one boiled potato. It was cheap and it was delicious.

On hot summer days we went to the Danube Canal and walked along the beautiful park that bordered its banks. We would stop at a tiny stand and get a "Gespritzter"-- a mixture of apple juice and mineral water. It tasted awfully good on a hot Sunday morning.

Other delicacies I enjoyed in my childhood, and for which I had a great yearning all though my life, were Marillen-Knoedel and Zwetschken-Knoedel. These were potato dough dumplings filled with an apricot or plums. When I (oh, so subtly) mentioned to my wife that I sure would like to have these dumplings "like my grandmother used to make them," she replied, "Then you go make them." And so I have. The potato dough has to be of perfect consistency to be rolled around an apricot or plum with a lump of sugar inside. Then they are plopped into softly boiling water until they rise to the top. Then they must be rolled in - what else -"Semmel Broesel" (buttered breadcrumbs). To top them off and make them perfect they were then sprinkled with powdered sugar. Oh, my! What a treat! All true Viennese salivate when one mentions Marillen or Zwetschken-Knoedel. I can remember my grandmother proudly carrying them out of the kitchen in a pointed heap on a platter. We had competitions to see who could eat the most.

Once in a great while I would go with my mother and father into downtown Vienna and we would stop in a little side street in the old part of the city right next to the Kohlmarkt and Graben which leads to St. Steven's Dome (Cathedral), where there was a tiny buffet restaurant called "Trzesniewski", which still exists today. It is always a great thrill to visit it and remember, especially with friends who find it an unusual and enchanting place. It serves little tiny finger sandwiches or canapés about the size of a silver dollar. The selection is just fantastic. One stands in front of the case and points. You take your selection along to the cash register, at which time you are asked if you want a vodka or a "Pfiff" to chase it. "Pfiff" means a whistle, but in "Trzesniewski" it means a little tiny glass of beer. Naturally, I didn't get either vodka or beer, but I would get some apple juice. Those sandwiches were just magnificent, and I imagine that I am not the only Viennese who remembers "Trzesniewski" and heads there at a fast trot at the first opportunity. It's my wife's favorite place for a pick-me-up in Vienna. She takes both a vodka and a "Pfiff!" The name of this restaurant is impossible to pronounce outside the borders of Poland, but in spite of this, most Viennese know it and struggle to say, "Gemma "Trzesniewski!" -- Let's go to Trzesniewski!"

  Then there were the wonderful afternoons when I would go with my grandmother or my mother to the coffee shops where I would be served my favorite things: an "Indianerkrapfen" -- a glazed pastry filled with coffee cream and a coffee glaze covering it; or a "Dobosch Torte," or "Schaumrolle" (a cream filled crispy roll). Ordering coffee, one is asked, "Mit Schlag" (with a "hit" of whipped cream on top.) One replies, "Bitte Mit" or "Danke Ohne" (without "Schlagobers.") Then the Napoleons!!!

    At home, of course, we had so many things. "Eingemachtes" -- a mixture of meat and sauces that can be warmed up over and over again, each time getting better. The wonderful "Eiernockerl" tiny dumplings made of egg dough. The famous "Kaiser Schmarrn" or "Emperor's Nothing," -- a kind of omelet torn into little pieces strewn with plum marmalade or one of berries. Then there was a "Reis Auflauff" -- cooked rice with milk and cinnamon. All children liked that.

    Once in a great while I would accompany my parents to one of the famous "Conditoreis" of Vienna that still exist today. There was Lehmann on the Graben and Dehmel's. Naturally, I also loved and still admire "Palatschinken," or "Nalesniki" in Poland, or "Palacinka" in Prague, Czechia, Slovakia, Croatia or Slovenia. This was Austro-Hungarian Empire cuisine. These thin pancakes all varied slightly as to filling, but basically were very similar. A thin dough pancake was rolled around farmer's cheese, berries, plums, and apples, sprinkled with powdered sugar and served with sour cream. In France they are called

"Crepes Suzette." If you are an adventurous tourist you can enjoy this fabulous cooking anywhere between Munich and Bucharest.

"Leberknoedelsuppe" (Liver dumpling soup) is a favorite all over the former Koeniglich und Kaiserliches Imperium. It took my wife a few years to get accustomed to eating some of these great specialties. Now, however, she cooks and serves them with great gusto, sometimes to the surprise and suspicion of our guests. One such dish is a very unique and famous Krakovian "Bigos" served in a particular restaurant on the main Marianski Plac in Krakow. Upon our return there many years later in the 1970's, lo and behold, there was the restaurant, and there was the "Bigos." This is a dish made with veal, beef, pork, and sausage flavored with sauerkraut and mushrooms, many herbs, and cooked in beer or wine. There were the wonderful pierogi, justly famous the world over. In Poland there was also access to good Jewish cooking, such as blintzes (the above Palatschinken), Gefilte fisch, and Matzo Ball Soup. I have a hard time deciding which I like better: Matzo Ball Soup or Leberknoedelsuppe. I could eat one or the other almost every day.

The contrast between the wonderful, nostalgic memories of childhood food favorites and the depravation and hunger I suffered during

World War II is indeed ironic, as is the subsequent over-abundance and over-indulgence in food after I came to live in the USA. Somehow this mirrors the history of the 20th Century.

CHAPTER 4

DR. HENRYK GLEISNER
A PIONEER OF THE POLISH FILM INDUSTRY

Dr. Henryk Gleisner was born in Krakow, one of 5 brothers and 3 sisters. His older brothers were Dr. Leon Gleisner, a well-known attorney in Krakow; and his partner in starting Muza Film in Warsaw Dr. Leopold Gleisner, also an attorney who graduated from the Jagellonian University in Krakow, as did Henryk.

Henryk was a genius, with great foresight. He was particularly entranced by the film industry, which was in its beginning. One of his most innovative achievements was importing about 1929 from Warner Brothers in Hollywood "The Jazz Singer" with Al Jolson. This was the first "Talkie" movie, though he had many silent movies in distribution before that. This, naturally, created some problems because the small movie theaters of Poland did not have the equipment necessary to play talking films. But, like everything else that progress brings, these things slowly got straightened out, and I presume that my Uncle Henryk probably made a fortune on his foresight.

At the beginning of 1930, Muza Film, in addition to distributing also started producing films. The films were relatively simplistic by today's standards. However, Muza Film was the most advanced production firm among many. They used specialists, artists, and experts in creating their films. This was also due to the modern, innovative approach of Henryk Gleisner.

Most of the films made were comedies; however, one of their most famous ones, "10 z Pawiaka" -- portrayed the Polish resistance against Russian rule (pre World War I) and a very famous prison break. Almost all films of Muza Films had a highly patriotic Polish content. Polish military regiments, songs, and a general glorification of Polish independence were the basis for many of the films.

Muza Film also owned a series of motion picture theaters. One of the largest in Poland was Kino Coliseum on Nowy Swiat in Warsaw, and nearby a smaller cinema, Kino Nowy Swiat. In Krakow there was Kino Wanda, also one in Katowice.

I met my Uncle Henryk on only two occasions: the first when our family went to visit Poland. We went first to Krakow and subsequently to Warsaw. Uncle Henryk showed us the offices of Muza Film located on Ulica Widok, a side street near the main thoroughfare of Warsaw, Marszalkowska, overlooking the center of the city. Light, large, clean rooms contained first an entry hallway and then the main offices with 6 desks, and on each end of this large room, the directors' offices. Henryk's office was neat and very well organized.

He showed us the back rooms, which contained a film projection room, with about 25 heavily upholstered lounge chairs and a large screen. While we were there, he ordered the projectionist to show us some of the latest "rushes." These were sequences of recently filmed scenes shot from different angles and for a variety of artistic reasons. The final shot would be selected by the director (regisseur.) The film was "Jadzia" with the then famous actress Jadwiga Smosarska, whom we met later at the film studios.

From there a small hall led to the laboratory. Here the films were shipped out as well as returned from the movie theaters, spooled back and checked for any breaks or damage to the perforations. Special machines did this. The main operator, who also doubled as a projectionist, was a tall gentleman named Wladislaw. His last name I never knew, but he was with Henryk from the very beginning and stayed on with Muza Film long after my father took over the direction of the firm.

From what I could observe, Henryk was a very well liked, popular bachelor. At several parties that we attended both at the film studios, as well as at his home, there were always a lot of beautiful young women dancing attendance on him.

The second time I met Uncle Henryk was when he came flying into Vienna by airplane in 1934 to the Aspen airport (which has not been a commercial airport for 50 years or more). It was very impressive to pick him up there, since not many people flew commercially in those days, and there were only about 6 passengers. We brought him back to our apartment in Vienna by taxi.

Not very long after that, we received a telephone call from Warsaw telling us that Uncle Henryk had succumbed to a fatal heart attack while taking a very hot bath, and Muza Film had lost its guiding genius. My other Uncle, Dr. Leopold Gleisner, had been stricken with Angina Pectoris and could not possibly take over the running of this firm. Since a few months earlier, my father, Jakob Gleisner, was permanently laid off from the Wiener Bankverein in Vienna, and had no way of finding another job, it was decided by the entire family that my father should come to Warsaw and take over the running of Muza Film. It was the midst of the depression and things were really rough and tough economically.

My father, Jakob, packed up his family and we moved to Warsaw, where we found a beautiful 4th floor apartment on Ulica Piekna (later Piusa

XI) overlooking the Koszykowa Market, always a bustling, lively view.

Although I was born in Vienna, my heritage includes several nationalities. On my mother's side, the family comes from Hungary and Romania; and my father, the brother of Henryk Gleisner, was born and raised in Krakow, Poland. So, I considered myself as a typical Viennese: a mixture of Poland, Hungary, of Jewish background. But when we came to Poland, I found myself to be a foreigner, though on my father's side I could certainly consider myself to be a Pole. We had Austrian passports, and shortly after our move in 1936, Austria was absorbed by Nazi Germany. Therefore we lost our Austrian passports and had to exchange them for German ones.

We had to present ourselves at the German Consulate located, ironically, on the same street as our apartment. It was decorated with the "Swastika" flags in every room, and a portrait of "The Fuehrer" Hitler. The new German passports contained a big red stamped **"J"** (Jude) on the front page. A new "middle name" was added. All Jewish women had the middle name of "Sarah" added; and all Jewish men, "Israel." This marking was requested by the Swiss authorities after the annexation of Austria. They informed the Germans that it was in their interests, if they wished to prevent Jews from leaving. It was also in Swiss interests to have visibly marked passports to distinguish between Jews, refugees, and visitors, since Jews were neither visitors or refugees and would not wish to leave Switzerland. The Swiss didn't want them.

Since we were foreigners from a hostile nation in Poland we had to report to the police every other month.

We had no great difficulties staying in Poland, thanks to my Uncle Dr. Leopold Gleisner, who was a Captain, during World War I in the Austrian Army. He participated in one of the bloodiest battles in World War I, the Battle of the Isonzo in Northern Italy. After he came back, he became a member of the Polish Legions under General Pilsudski. As a "Legionnaire" he had considerable influence. He helped us to stay in Poland, and I consider the hospitality that we received at that time as unforgettable.

Dr. Leopold Gleisner was also President of the Chamber of Commerce of the Polish Film Industry and on the government Film Advisory Board of the Interior Ministry.

While we found a haven, at best temporarily, many thousands of Jews were trying to escape from Austria and Germany and found no way to get out. Virtually all the world closed its borders to these unfortunate refugees.

The rolls of film sent out to motion picture theaters were made from so-called "lavender copies." These originals were very costly and valuable. They were stored in a safe warehouse in Mokotow near Warsaw. Not long after our escape from Warsaw, we found out that they were destroyed in a German dive-bombing attack by "Stuka" bombers (Sturz Kampf Flugzeug) in the early part of the war. Consequently, all thirteen motion pictures created and produced by Muza Film are probably lost forever.

In 1938 one of the biggest film events in Warsaw was the showing of the French film, Jean Renoir's "Grand Illusion" at the Coliseum movie theater for many weeks. Since Warsaw was permeated with Nazi sympathizers and spies shortly before the outbreak of World War II, the distribution of this anti-militaristic film did not escape attention of German Authorities. This movie was declared "Cinema Enemy #1" by Nazi propaganda minister Josef Goebbels. The negative was later confiscated by the Germans after their occupation of France, and thought to be lost. Eventually, fifty years later, it resurfaced in the U.S.S.R. It is today considered as one of the great treasures of the cinema.

In 1971 my wife and I visited Poland. While in Warsaw seeing all the sights we came to the old Pawiak Prison. Before World War I, this prison housed some Polish revolutionaries caught during protests against the oppressive Czarist regime. At that time there was a famous prison break of 10 prisoners. Muza Film made a movie of it. In the Pawiak Prison, to my greatest astonishment I saw large photographs depicting some scenes of the movie "The Ten Out of The Pawiak.

THE FOLLOWING MOVIE THEATERS BELONGED TO MUSA FILM IN POLAND

Kino Coliseum - Nowy Swiat - Warsaw
Kino Nowy Swiat - Nowy Swiat - Warsaw
Kino Wanda - Krakow
Kino ?   - Katowice

<u>MUZA FILM MOTION PICTURE PRODUCTION</u>
Following is a short description of the 13 films produced by Muza Film:
(Many records show the name of the firm as "Blok Muza Film.")

1930 - Janko Muzykant (Janko the Musician)
         This film was probably the most popular Polish film shown in other countries.

1931 - Dziesieciu z Pawiaka (Ten out of the Pawiak)

    The sound strip for this film was made in Berlin. The script was based on the memories of a participant of an actual armed action of the Polish resistance movement in 1906 that resulted in the breakout of ten prisoners. They were incarcerated for anti Czarist and anti Russian armed rebellion. At the Gala Premiere in Warsaw, General Pilsudski, the "Generalissimo" of Poland, with his daughters, the President of the Republic of Poland, Moscicki, various ministers, a host of generals of the high command, as well as the entire diplomatic corps attended. This film gathered many prizes and awards, the gold medal of the weekly magazine "Kino." It was sold to the United States and was the first Polish film shown on Broadway titled, "The Condemned." It was also widely distributed in South America.

1932 - Ksiezna Lowicka (Duchess Lowicka)

    The first costume picture on a grand scale based on an historical novel. It was sold and distributed in South America as well as other countries.

1932 - Ulani, Ulani, Chlopcy Malowani (Ulans, Painted Boys)

A farcical comedy. This film was very profitable, was sold to the U. S. A., Czechoslovakia, and Palestine.

1933 - Przybleda (The Vagabond)
A folkloric film about the life of the Huculs, a gypsy-type tribe.

1933 - Kazdemu Wolno Kochac (Everyone May Love)
A comedy, one of the first sound movies produced in Poland. Distributed also in South America.

1933 - Szpieg W Masce (The Masked Spy)
A sensational spy movie.

1933 - Wyrok Zycia (Life Sentence)
A film about social ambitions. All critics declared it as the most advanced film of the 1933-34 season. Received a major award in Berlin where a Festival Opening took place in 1935. It was also distributed in many other countries.

1934 - Sluby Ulanskie (Ulan Weddings)
A comedy depicting military maneuvers. The German distributor also sold it to Germany and to other countries.

1934 - Czy Lucyna To Dziewczyna? (Is Lucyna a Girl?)
    A comedy also sold to Germany and by the German distributor to other countries.
(This was a type of "Tootsie" movie with Dustin Hoffman.)

1935 - Dwie Joasie (Two Joasias)
    A Cinderella story transposed into modern times.

1936 - Jadzia (Jadzia)
    A funny love story about two representatives of competing sporting goods firms.

1936 - Jego Wielka Milosc (His Great Love)
    A dramatic fable was written specially for a famous actor, Stefan Jaracz. It was shown in Germany and the distributor sold it to other countries.

    After the death of Henry Gleisner, Muza Film did not produce any further movies. The depression deprived the firm of the necessary capital to produce. Consequently, my father, Jakob Gleisner, conducted only the distribution, and in early 1939, the firm was liquidated.
    Muza Film gathered the most outstanding directors, artists and actors of both stage and film available in Poland in the 1930's. Original music was composed. A long list of these outstanding

co-workers can be found in the archives, as well as in the Polish "Who's Who."

CHAPTER 5

GYMNASIUM HOZA #76

Upon our arrival in Warsaw neither my mother nor I spoke Polish. I was given very intensive instruction with morning and afternoon tutors in Polish as well as all school subjects at the same time. In addition, I continued with my French lessons and also went twice a week to the British Consulate for English lessons. This was a difficult time for a young fellow, but I understood the need, and for some reason I found satisfaction and pleasure in acquiring the necessary languages and knowledge.

After three months I passed an entrance exam into a State Gymnasium (high school) and was accepted. I immediately made many friends among the pupils as well as with the teachers. There was a certain amount of leeriness or distance shown by some of the people for various reasons. To begin with, I was considered an Austrian. The Poles considered the Austrians as Germans, which was a nation very much at odds with Poland. Others, of course, knew that I was Jewish. That created a lot of confusion. In any case, I was a stranger.

One of my best friends was Wojtek, a tall, slim son of an officer in the Polish Army. We became good friends, going bicycling together, helping one another with school subjects (he wasn't very good with mathematics, and I was a little better, so I helped him with that; while he helped me with my language difficulties). One of the subjects was the equivalent of R.O.T.C. A Lieutenant of the Polish Army in full uniform came once a week and gave us military instruction. We had a small shooting range in the basement of our school. The targets were paper propped up against sandbags. We used 22 caliber rifles.

    The first few classes were very awkward because the Lieutenant wasn't sure that he should include a foreigner, a non-Polish citizen, who actually carried a **German** passport, to participate in Polish reserve officer's training instruction. My friend Wojtek jumped to my rescue. To my greatest astonishment, he stood up and told the class, including the Lieutenant, that I was a persecuted refugee from Germany, more opposed to the Germans, with good reasons, than any of the others in the class. He persuaded the Lieutenant to include me along with everyone else in this program. This helped me a great deal because I had a little bit of practice in target shooting, and I was one of the better shots. I was also very diligent and careful to make sure that I didn't step on anyone's toes. When it was all done, I came out with a very good grade, an A, and there were no further discussions about my background.

CHAPTER 6

A FAREWELL TO THE DRAFT HORSES

The weather conditions in September 1939 were the most beautiful in Europe since many years. Each day was sunny and warm and the nights were very pleasant.

We arrived in Warsaw by train from a summer resort called Krynica in the south of Poland, on the 31st of August. My school was to start within a few days. We had a considerable amount of luggage, but we took only one small suitcase along with us that evening, my father saying he would get the rest of the luggage from the railway station the next day.

However, that next morning, a beautiful blue skied summer day, several formations of German Stuka attack bombers appeared on the horizon, flew over Warsaw, and bombed the hell out of the Warsaw railway station (and, incidentally, all the Gleisner family vacation luggage). World War II had begun.

Shortly thereafter, the situation in Warsaw became decidedly frantic and chaotic. The perfect weather conditions, naturally, were very helpful for the rapid advance of the German invaders toward the Capital. The Polish Army fell apart, the defense minister had a German girlfriend (who was a spy), and the entire air force of Poland was bombed out of existence within 24 hours, because, of course, the Germans knew the location of every airplane.

The Polish government broadcast a warning that civilians should leave Warsaw because fighting was imminent. After my father received several telephone calls from friends, we packed our things and left for the suburb of Mokotow, where we met with our friends. I remember a nice old gentleman, Mr. Landman, and his wife particularly because Mrs. Landman had an enormous bust...which turned out to be where all the family jewelry was hidden. Also among our friends were the families Glocer and Czarnozyl.

One of the families had negotiated for a flat farm wagon with rubber tires, with bales of straw around the outside, and loose straw in the middle. To it were hitched two magnificent draft horses.

The whole company, including the owner of the draft horses, took off toward the east. For me as a young boy this was a rather pleasant experience -- an adventure. I did not realize that I would not see Warsaw again for a long time, nor that I would ever see my home again.

The splendid horses were shod with heavy studs and with large pieces of automobile tires incorporated into their shoes to diminish the shock of constantly working on hard, paved roads. Often during the journey we were passed by military traffic, and several times we had to jump into the roadside ditch to avoid the low flying German planes which were machine gunning everything that moved on the road. The two horses stood quietly in spite of all the havoc around them, and luckily were never injured. We drove all day and at night we always found a little barn or farmhouse where we asked if we could stay overnight. We bought eggs, milk and bread, paying a rather generous price, and it always worked out. We traveled in this manner for about a week.

On September 10th as we approached the River Bug, we decided to continue going because the weather was so good and we wanted to cover a little more distance. We approached the bridge, which was still intact, and advanced into a small village at approximately 10:00 in the evening. We started to look around for a place to quarter and take care of the horses. We found a farmhouse and talked to the owner, who was quite willing to let us use his barn, where we bedded down in the straw, spreading blankets for our beds. The driver took care of the horses, and we all drifted off to sleep.

Upon waking the next morning, we found that the first units of the Soviet Red Army had occupied the town.

We didn't know at the time, but the Germans had concluded the Ribbentrop-Molotov Pact and, as happened in past history, sliced Poland into two pieces. The western part was absorbed into the "Reich" and "General Government." The eastern parts were incorporated into the Byelorussian and Ukrainian Soviet Republics.

We read placards posted by the Soviet Military Command (in Ukrainian and Polish): "For 3 days anyone wishing to cross the bridge and go to the western part of Poland will be permitted to do so without military inspection." Thereafter, a regular border-crossing procedure would be in force.

The Warsaw owner of the wagon and horses naturally wanted to get back to his family and home. Everyone chipped in and paid him for his work, equipment, and horses, which we all felt had saved the lives of our little group. Thanking him profusely, we sadly bid him good-by. It was particularly heart-rending for me to part with those two fine draft horses. I petted them a lot, and fed them bits of bread and sugar on the sly without anyone seeing, for those commodities were very precious and in extremely short supply. It was my "farewell" to the Warsaw draft horses.

Perhaps my later great love for horses began with these patient and magnificent draft horses, which carried us away from war torn Warsaw.

1940 IN LWOW AT HIGH SCHOOL

CHAPTER 7

UNDER SOVIET OCCUPATION
A SOVIET "LESSON"

The Capital of the eastern part of Poland, called Galicia, was Lwow. The Austrians that occupied this part of the world prior to World War I called the city Lemberg. It had a very rich past, with a center of Polish inhabitants strongly interspersed with Jews, who mainly belonged to the commercial part of the city, but also influenced the universities, sciences, and some of the free professions. The outskirts, the countryside, and the outlying districts were predominantly Ukrainian.

It was difficult for me to understand, even as a youngster, why the Free Polish Republic, which was created by Marshall Pilsudski after World War I, would pursue a relatively intolerant policy toward its minorities, such as the Ukrainians. It would have been far wiser to accommodate them and show cooperation and support, especially in view of the fact that the Polish people themselves had been persecuted for centuries -- their country had been sliced up and divided by the three great powers, Russia, Germany and Austria, time and again -- by the Austrians in a more liberal way, by the Germans much less so, but by the Russians in a regime of oppression that can only be compared to modern day dictatorships.

In any case, I found myself in Lwow in September of 1939. The Red Army had overrun the eastern part of Poland, and the Germans the western part. They divided Poland between themselves, signing the infamous Ribbentrop-Molotov Pact, and pledged "non-aggression," which lasted about a year.

Our family was satisfied to be in the Soviet part of Poland, because the Germans instituted a reign of terror on their side that was directed with the greatest ferocity against the Jews; but openly declared anyone of Polish origin as an "Untermensch" or a substandard human being who did not have ANY rights or considerations toward education, work, or even survival.

The so-called "General Gouvernment" instituted by the Germans had its seat in the Wawel Castle of the ancient Polish Kings in Krakow. The Governor, a man by the name of Hans Frank, was eventually hanged in Nuremberg during the War Crimes Trials. The partly announced (and partly unannounced) official policy of the Hitlerian government was to work the Poles to death and ultimately exterminate them -- and above all annihilate their culture and their language.

As far as the Jews were concerned, there was a "rapid" solution being sought -- meaning their <u>immediate</u> extermination. The same applied to the gypsies, due to racist writings by a Hitlerian theoretician, named Rosenberg.

After the tremendous turmoil of the outbreak of World War II in September 1939, my father, mother and I found ourselves in Lwow. This ancient city of 800,000 population had swollen to about twice or three times its size by the influx of refugees. Those that came were usually of a higher income bracket and of higher education. Those people didn't sit still, but wanted to get out from under the Hitlerian regime. They included a part of the intelligentsia of Warsaw as well as of Krakow, both of Polish as well as of Jewish origin. The town was very much "alive" and the Russian occupiers had a difficult time governing because the sophistication of the new population was so much greater than the Russians' background and education. Jokes abounded about how Russian officers occupying houses or apartments did not know how to use a toilet, and thought it was a strange type of washbowl; and how they tried to pretend that they had western amenities at home somewhere in Usbekistan, or even in the European parts of the Soviet Union, such as in some cities of the Urals.

This created a very strange relationship between occupiers and occupied people. The Occupied Poles, and for that matter the Ukrainians, felt themselves so far superior to their Soviet occupiers that a mutual dislike and observance of distance resulted. There was hardly any fraternizing between Soviet officials, military, and civilian and indigenous or refugee population, even though Russian policy was to accomplish that.

I went to gymnasium (high school) on Sapiehy Street. We still had our old teachers, called "Professors" who were left over from the Polish Republic. The school principal was a Soviet woman of rather tremendous physical proportions, who spoke only Russian.

We continued with our studies and it was interesting that during this one year, we had a subject called "The History of the Communist Party of the Soviet Union," discussed in a book that was printed on extremely cheap paper. We all wondered why this was the case, because all the other schoolbooks were done on a much better quality paper. After about 6 months we had to give back these books, and we were issued new editions of "The History of the Communist Party, etc." "History" was being changed in Moscow. Certain people became "non-persons," while others were described in more glorious terms.

This, of course, had to do with the changes of policy, which constantly took place, and the whims, power plays and murders of Stalin.

Naturally, the regular teachers were not convinced Communists and in effect, some were very anti-Communist. Several professors would not suppress their Polish nationalism, although everyone was afraid of the consequences, knowing full well that the Stalinist regime and the close scrutiny of the secret police (which was then called the NKVD) would not permit any open discussion or criticism in any manner of any part of the Soviet State.

Suddenly, in the middle of a weekday during classroom hours, the entire student population of 400 was called to a general assembly of all students and professors into the aula, which was a large assembly hall on the 4th and top floor of our school. At the head table sat the large lady Principal along with several government officials, some of whom were in Soviet uniforms. Several Russians stood along the walls. We could identify them by the visors on their caps, which were rectangular, whereas the local ones were rounded...so we could recognize Russians from a mile away by the way they were dressed. The clothing industry of the Soviet Union was and is nothing to brag about!

During the course of the speeches it was pointed out that many class enemies, people's enemies, and enemies of the Soviet State were among us. The speeches were inflammatory and exhorted the elimination of these enemies. After a short while a regular riot broke out. Those "types" standing along the walls created it. They were screaming and beating people over their heads with chair legs. The doors were blocked by more of these obvious plainclothesmen, but most of the students fought their way to escape.

After I got out into the street, I realized that the chair legs carried by the Russians were all light colored, whereas our school had only dark stained chairs. Those "types" were agents of the NKVD planted at the meeting, and they had brought along their own chair legs for their "work." In the process of this, many of our pupils were severely injured, but two of our professors were killed, having their heads crushed in.

This was only one of many experiences with Totalitarian systems, and I would never forget them.

During this time a pervasive fear was evident in all layers of the population, mainly created by the overwhelming and overriding powers of the N.K.V.D. meaning Narodni Komisariat Wnutrich Del (Peoples Komisariat of Internal Affairs). It was the secret police, but not only the secret police. They also had uniformed units, and they had their own military regiments, their own cars, trucks, tanks, artillery, and barracks. The N.K.V.D. was all-powerful. It was called shortly before that M.V.D. and before that it was the G.P.U., and Before the Bolshevik Revolution they had the same thing during the Czarist times called the Ochrana. Russia has always been governed by a lawless, overpowering type of police apparatus. The N.K.V.D. arrested people without any kind of warrant and without apparent reason. We tried to figure out just why they had arrested someone. Everyone fearfully anticipated the knock on the door during the night. The people were arrested and were never heard of again. They just simply disappeared.

    They arrested all known officers of the Polish Army. Later it was discovered that the officers were brought to the Forest of Katyn near Smolensk. With their hands tied behind them, several thousand were all summarily executed with a shot to the back of the heads. When the Germans discovered this, they invited international observers to examine the massacre. However the Soviets blamed this butchery upon the Germans. After the War the truth leaked out. The affair of the Katyn atrocity is so well known in Poland that the remembrance of this particular barbarity has prevented Poland from having good relations with Russia for many decades, and will probably continue so for the foreseeable future.

Constant waves of arrest and deportations were ongoing in Lwow. A neighbor of my Uncle Stefan's who lived in central Lwow came to tell us that Stefan had been arrested during the night and was GONE! Of course, we did not know for what reason or where he was held, or anything else. We tried to make inquiries at the police, but were met with arrogant silence and no answers. We were simply told that he was arrested by the N.K.V.D. and that was the end of information.

The future looked very bleak. The Stalinist terror encompassed all walks of live. We were always afraid to be overheard. Anyone who criticized the regime was a suspected provocateur. This situation prevailed even in our school. My father tried to communicate by mail with some distant cousins in the United States to obtain an affidavit to leave via the Trans Siberian Railway to Shanghai, China, and thence to immigrate to the U. S. This escape route was used by a few Jewish families and was a very tenuous but possible way. The mails were very slow, and as time wore on, nothing came of it. In June 1941 when the Germans attacked the Soviet Union, everything came to a halt.

Prior to June '41 it was interesting to observe the amount of train traffic that went through Lwow westward toward the Germans. On the basis of the Ribbentrop-Molotov Pact, the Soviet Union helped Germany with all kinds of raw materials, food, and war supplies. The trains never ceased running westward. It was astounding to us because the Soviet Union itself was short of various basic supplies and certain foods were almost unobtainable, such as sugar, butter, and some other scarce commodities. Yet, at the same time, the Soviets, particularly Stalin personally, deluded themselves that they could avoid a confrontation with the Germans by helping them.

Shortly after the German attack in August 1941, walking through Lwow I witnessed the mass of Soviet prisoners of war (about 10,000 of them) being marched through the city toward some camp. Their condition was deplorable. They were obviously starved, some were badly wounded, but despite their condition they were just driven on by German soldiers through the city. The sight was incomprehensible. The cruelty of the German **Army (NOT** the Gestapo or other security forces) was evident. It was also clear that the Germans had no great intentions of taking care of these prisoners of war. As it turned out they died by the millions. It is not well known that the losses and sacrifices by the Russian people during World War II were so overwhelming, that there isn't a single Russian family who hasn't lost some members during these hostilities. It was estimated at the time that 40 million Russians died during World War II.

    All shreds of legality were abandoned. What was not worth plundering or was too cumbersome to move, was destroyed. Czechoslovakia was stripped -- not just art, but trolley buses, cotton, iron and food, entire libraries, scientific laboratories. Then Poland -- picked clean in 6 months -- the National Museums of Warsaw and Krakow, the cathedral of Lublin, homes of Polish nobility, university libraries, and monasteries.

    If the Poles were considered barbarians, the Russians were considered scarcely human, so Russia was plundered with considerable brutality. Until the Revolution in 1918, Russia had been one of the richest countries in the world in terms of art. Handsomely endowed cities, monasteries, museums and churches were filled with centuries of superb craftsmanship and careful collecting commissioned by the Czars and nobility. During the Revolution collections were abandoned or sold by fleeing owners for ridiculously low prices, or by the state. Yet, Rosenberg, Hitler's facilitator of "the greatest art operation in history," (read: art theft) and his men found museum collections beyond all dreams, so much that a "special formation" under Foreign Minister von Ribbentrop was given the task of keeping close behind the advancing troops, ready to secure and seize "all cultural treasures and all objects of great historic value, valuable books and films, and to dispatch them to Germany." Freight trains of 50 wagons piled high with booty reached Germany every month. It was not until after the war that the world really learned how devastating had been the German policy towards the Russian Cultural history. Secret orders were found of plans to annihilate some cities. "The Fuehrer has decided to erase from the face of the earth St. Petersburg." The magnificent Baroque palaces of St. Petersburg, known throughout the world for their furniture, porcelain, Gobelin tapestries, marble busts, pictures and painted silk hangings, were totally destroyed.

  The story of the disappearance of the amber room, one of the most valued possessions of the Soviet Union, taken from the Catherine Palace at Tsarskoe Selo is one of the most celebrated and puzzling art thefts of all time, yet to be solved. The Hitlerite vandals seemed to take particular pleasure in desecrating what they could not carry away. Priceless books were used as paving stones. In a frenzy of destruction, Russia was laid waste. By 1944, 427 museums had been totally destroyed, palaces and pavilions, houses and libraries pillaged, and blown up. 1670 Orthodox churches torn down. The cultural heritage of Russia was reduced to rubble. More than 1700 towns, and 70,000 villages were left in ruins, 32,000 factories blown up, 100,000 collective farms demolished. The sheer brutality of the German destruction of the Soviet Union was important for what was to follow.

At Yalta the three leaders of the Allies accepted a secret protocol -- that it was only fair that compensation should go to those who had carried the main burden of the war, and suffered the worst losses. The Russians had lost 8 million in battle and 20 million more through German oppression, starvation and hardship. Their country had been pillaged and laid waste by the Germans. Russia had serious reparations in mind. May and June of 1945 saw Berlin stripped and vandalized. Power plugs, door handles, entire factories were dismantled and trained back to Russia to replace those smashed by the Germans. Technology: typewriters to telephones were particularly prized. Russian soldiers combed through the ruins, smashing everything they could not take away. European masterpieces, already looted once by the Germans buffeted about in the backs of lorries, and were moved yet again, this time never to reappear.

At the time of the Stalinist terror in Lwow there was an extraordinary number of suicides. The people who knew they were on the list to be arrested by the N.K.V.D. committed suicide because it was known that in the cellars of the police and N.K.V.D. stations people were tortured to death.

Since there was a great lack of gasoline or diesel fuel, there were two types of transportation in Lwow: streetcars which were running very heavily overcrowded, and droshki -- horse drawn carriages. The only people who were openly critical of the Soviets and voiced their opinions in a loud manner were the drivers of the droshki. For some reason nothing happened to them. They made disparaging remarks about the Russians and about the Stalinist administration.

I had a very frightening experience. Shortly after the Germans marched into Lwow, it was decreed that all Jewish people had to wear armbands with the blue Star of David. I did not submit at the beginning because the terror and enforcement of the various orders was not yet organized and functioning. Jewish people were not allowed to use any type of public transportation, such a streetcars. I used the streetcars regularly. There was also a regulation that you could not hang on the steps of the streetcar, but in the case of overcrowding you had to wait for the next one. They were all very overcrowded. A Ukrainian policeman took me off the steps where I was hanging, and marched me into the station. Without a further word, he pushed me into a cell in the cellar and closed the door. I was in a panic! I was afraid they would discover I was Jewish Then I would have a serious "problem." The penalty was always DEATH for sabotaging a German order.

After brooding there for perhaps an hour, I walked up to the door to look out through the little peephole to see what was going on. To my greatest astonishment, I found the door unlocked. I opened it and silently snuck up the few steps to reconnoiter. While the policeman at the desk was not looking, I slithered out onto the street and was gone. I think the policeman thought only to scare me into abiding by the rules; and I was just plain lucky!

CHAPTER 8

AUSTRIAN GALICIA, EASTERN POLAND, WESTERN UKRAINE

After our exit from war-torn Warsaw we wound up in Lwow { in Ukrainian it is Lwiw} [formerly the Austrian city of Lemberg]. Shortly after arriving in Lwow we found a good-sized room on the first floor in a nice, clean house on Grodecka Street in which we arranged ourselves in relative comfort. My mother, though, was extremely unhappy because we had left all our possessions in Warsaw. My father took only a few gold coins and a couple of small suitcases with personal belongings. All the rest was left.

In Warsaw we had a luxurious apartment, with two bedrooms, two living rooms, bath, kitchen and auxiliary rooms. Evening parties and gatherings held at our apartment were memorable. It was about 5 minutes walk away from the Warsaw Polytechnic University. A bit further were the open fields that held the Warsaw racetrack. Various members of our family lived in this general section, so there was a lot of visiting among us.

I especially remember an evening gala party where my handsome cousin Olek, an officer's candidate, appeared in his magnificent Polish uniform, impressing the ladies tremendously. There was dancing lasting until the early morning hours. I suppose one of the reasons I remember so well is that I couldn't go to sleep because of all the noise and revelry.

    The history of the city of Lwow is very interesting. It is a very old city -- the records go back to the 12th century. It was the seat of several Polish kings, above all Kazimierz the Great, whose castle still stands there. It was also a center for many cultural buildings and museums, among which was the famous Panorama Raclawicka, situated today in the city of Wroclaw. It was taken away by the Soviets, and after lengthy negotiations was finally given back to postwar Poland.

    The city, a crossroads between the east and west, also had economic ties with Turkey. In the Middle Ages, particularly under the Kingdom of Zygmunt, it attracted a lot of Jews who contributed to its cultural and economic development. In 1772 Austria occupied Lwow (or Lemberg), and it became part of the Austro-Hungarian Empire after the division of Poland among the three powers -- Germany, Austria, and Russia. After the peace of 1809 between Napoleon and Austria, it was officially incorporated into the Austrian Empire, and in 1815 during the Vienna Congress, it also became the capital of the

Province of Galicia. The Austrian influence shows strongly in the architecture, as well as in the metropolitan character of the city in the 20th Century, up until the Soviet occupation.

In the pre World War I years between 1900 and 1918, the political life of Lwow was very lively. It was the seat of pronounced political activity on the part of the Polish independence movement. The countryside surrounding the city of Lwow was completely Ukrainian, and that also held true for the years between the wars under independent Poland between 1918 and 1939. The Ukrainian nationalists were for the most part strongly anti Polish. Unfortunately the Polish government was never able to change this situation to a more friendly relationship with the Ukrainian minority.

In the pre World War I years the population was around 207,000 of which there were 101,000 Roman Catholics (about 51%), Greek Orthodox 34,000 (17%), and Jewish 57,000 (29%).

As World War I came to an end in 1918 fighting broke out between the Polish and Ukrainian populations. During the 1920 war of Poland against the Soviet Union, the cavalry of the Soviets under General Budjonny came as far as the suburbs of Lwow. But shortly thereafter the Poles chased the Soviets back all the way to Kiev; a great victory for Poland, and a tremendous loss for the Red Army (a fact invariably suppressed thereafter in the history books of the Soviets).

Between the two world wars, Lwow became a center of science and culture and also economic well-being. On the 22nd of September, 1939 the Russian Army occupied Lwow in accordance with the arrangement with the Germans in a pact made between Stalin and Hitler, commonly known as the Molotov-Ribbentrop Pact. Immediately thereafter deportations and exterminations of nationalist elements, mainly Polish ones, took place; but the Soviets also arrested quite a few Ukrainian nationalists they felt were not in favor of the Soviet system.

Since a lot of the refugees streamed into Lwow, as my family did, the population of Lwow was greatly enlarged. It was estimated that the total amount of refugees in the area in Lwow amounted to somewhere between 160 and 180 thousand people. Altogether, from that time until June of 1941, at which time the Soviets withdrew to the east under the onslaught of the German Army, the Soviets in the area of Lwow and the adjoining province had arrested and transported away approximately 400,000 persons. We did not know at the time about the purges the Soviets committed against the Polish and the Jewish intelligentsia, teachers, and officers. About 4000 Polish officers as well as officials, teachers, professors and community leaders disappeared. The officers were murdered near Smolensk in the infamous woods of Katyn, executed **by the Soviet NKVD, the Soviet secret police).** This was the one exception to the many massacres in which the Germans did **not** participate. However, after the War it was proven without any doubt that this action was done on orders of Stalin, and is well documented as one of the most heinous crimes in Soviet history.

During these arrests and murderous activities, the population was frightened and terrorized. For instance on the 22nd of August, 1942, 300 people who were under suspicion of working with the Polish underground were arrested, and it was quite common that people were just put against a wall on the Strzelecki Plac and shot. When the Germans moved in the arrests and shootings of course continued, directed now mostly against the Jewish population, although the Polish population were also victims.

One of the first results of this political terror also touched our family. Shortly after we arrived in Lwow we met with Uncle Stefan in a small rented room. He was a deactivated officer of the Polish Army. It wasn't very long before he just disappeared. At the time Stefan was arrested by the Soviet authorities, we didn't know about the massacre of the Polish officers at Katyn. It turned out after the War that he had been particularly lucky that he was not shipped to Katyn. He was transported to Kazakhstan and spent the rest of the war in a gulag (prison camp) building railroad tracks. It was back breaking work under very poor conditions but he survived. In a strange twist of fate, our friends, the family Landesman, were transported to the same camp. Uncle Stefan, a confirmed bachelor prior to the outbreak of the war, married Manja Landesman out in Kazakhstan. I discovered this in 1950 and was able to help them somewhat while they were in Tel Aviv living on Dizingoff Street.

    In 1955 on my way between Tokyo and Munich, I had a stopover in Tel Aviv and had a wonderful visit with both my Uncle Stefan and his wife, Manja. We talked about a lot of things, but we did not mention much the Holocaust experiences we both went through. I was then, and many years thereafter, very reticent in talking about what I had seen and experienced. This, I understand now, is not unusual. Most of the Holocaust survivors have gone through this same phase.

    In 1942 the Germans shipped out 15,000 Jews. Most likely all were murdered in Belzec and cremated there. Belzec was held in such secrecy that no exact figures are available even today. During the same year they created the Ghetto and compressed 45,000 Jewish people into this small area. On January, 1944 there were 12,000 in the Ghetto, and in the Janowska concentration camp, there were 15,000. In August of 1944 of this total there were 800 persons left. The constant political terror under the Soviets prepared me mentally for the oncoming onslaught of the German terror and persecution. The Soviets ruled through the headquarters of the NKVD. It was a whole separate state within a state. They had their own army, their own secret police, and their own uniformed troops. Their headquarters were very near our high school on Sapiehy Street across from a convent. It was guarded like a fortress and no one could even walk on the sidewalk of this building. The population, regardless of nationality, was all afraid and terrorized by them. Constant executions took place in the inner courtyard.

    Oddly enough the persecution and terror were primarily directed toward politics or imaginary politics, which was typical of the Stalin regime. For instance, black marketing was tolerated and the laws were not very strictly applied.

    After school in the evenings I spent a lot of time in the coffee houses around Plac Mariacki because that was where the black market operated. I traded coins and currency, gold, silver, watches, precious stones -- all kinds of commodities. And that is what kept us alive and going.

At about that time we had some strange news about our apartment in Warsaw. We had a maid, a Polish girl, Veronika. She was probably 5 feet tall, very thin and small, and was not very good looking. Consequently, she had a hard time finding a boyfriend and never went out during her days off. While we were in Lwow we heard that she got married and was leading a very happy life, probably aided by the fact that she "inherited" our apartment and all our possessions: Persian carpets, my mother's jewelry, silver, a stack of U.S. $20.00 gold coins, furniture, appliances, clothing....**everything!**

My father began dispatching letters for help to various distant relatives in the United States. Some of the people who had affidavits from the United States were allowed to leave via the Trans Siberian Railway, and they went to Shanghai, China, and from there across to Mexico or to the United States. One of our friends escaped that way. Unfortunately, we never received an affidavit -- for our family an inevitable path to disaster.

Hoping to receive this affidavit, we applied to emigrate, and were therefore issued so-called "Stateless" identity papers. As a result of that we had to report to the infamous NKVD periodically;

each time with a great amount of nervous fear, wondering if we would ever come out again. There we sat and waited for an interminable amount of time, and eventually, after having answered a few perfunctory questions, our papers were stamped and we were shown our way out.

CHAPTER 9

IN LWOW UNDER THE SOVIET OCCUPATION 1939 - 1941

Under the Soviet administration (1939-41) the supply of food was very sporadic and unpredictable. Food stamps were issued, but most of them could never be redeemed. One had to stand long hours in lines. If one saw a line forming in front of a (government) store, one got into the line, and only later did one find out what was available. I understand that this situation did not change very much for as long as the Soviet Union existed, with the possible exception of Moscow and Leningrad, where the supply was and is somewhat better.

During that time, however, we did not suffer too badly because the black market flourished, and since my parents could not cope with this kind of situation, I became rather expert at dealing in the black market.

We survived these times because when we left Warsaw, my father had prudently taken along with him a few gold coins. These were changed for dollar paper money, because one did not want to have too many Rubles on hand when exchanging a valuable $20.00 gold piece. The

$20.00 gold piece was exchanged for approximately $50.00 paper, and the paper dollars had to be in denominations of $10's and $5's, and above all, singles. Strangely, the Soviet police generally did not interfere with black market activities.

    A single dollar banknote was exchanged for somewhere around 400 to 700 Rubles, depending on the news on the BBC to which we listened every evening. Our family could survive rather well on a single dollar every week, by adding black market food to our meager food stamp supplies.

    In addition to this I was also busy after school hours wheeling and dealing in watches and jewelry, or any other commodity that presented possibilities of making a few Rubles. For a short time, I was also a part time insurance salesman for the Government Insurance Corporation of the Soviet Union. The sales were almost nil because no one expected the Soviets to last long enough in that part of the world for them to be able to cash in on an insurance policy. The people were right! The Soviet occupation of Eastern Poland lasted less than 2 years. On June 22, 1941 the Germans invaded the Soviet Union and occupied Eastern Poland within hours. War anew!

    The moment the Germans came in it became extremely hazardous to listen to foreign broadcasts, such as the BBC -- strictly a case for the death penalty! We continued to listen nevertheless. Every evening we posted sentries to watch for police or strangers near our "apartments."

After the Soviets moved ahead and took the eastern part of Poland, while the Germans occupied the western part, there was a year of peace. I went to school and had two very close friends with whom I spent a lot of time. One was Norbert Landa (called Nolek) and the other was Anatol Schwieger (Tolek), the son of a medical doctor, whose wife was also a doctor. We were often together and went to the movies, played poker and chess, and in general became very good friends.

By the time the Germans advanced again and occupied Lwow, our friend Nolek had disappeared with his family. We are almost sure that they moved east toward Moscow, because their family had a brother-in-law who was in a high position in the transport ministry commissariat of the Soviets in Moscow. He had visited with them, so we knew of the connection. Therefore, Tolek and I assumed that the family Landa had fled and probably saved their lives.

Tolek's father, upon the renewed occupation under the Germans, obtained Costa Rica passports, and the family was interned by the Gestapo. The treatment was reasonably good. For a long period of time Tolek lived with his parents and sister in a house, which they could not leave. They were internees, virtually prisoners.

Later on that year I tried to visit with him, and he did come to the window; but we couldn't talk. He waved me away because he was afraid that I would be caught by the Gestapo, who were guarding this house. At that time I didn't have false papers, and I was running around without a Jewish armband, for which there was the death penalty.

They were transferred from internment into a concentration camp. In 1945 they were marched westward because the S.S. prisoner guards wanted to avoid being captured by the Soviet Red Army. Finally, after many prisoners died of exhaustion, Tolek talked the guards into leaving the prisoners there and fleeing in order to save their own lives. Within the next 48 hours the American Army liberated them. They were slowly nursed back to life.

We lost contact. In 1957 I attended the National Sporting Goods Show in Chicago. In the evening we walked to a nearby restaurant, the Swiss Village. While entering through a revolving door, another couple exited. We stopped -- transfixed! I yelled, "Tolek, is that YOU?," as he said the same to me. We embraced and were very overcome by our emotions. From then on we kept in touch, until his death a few years ago, and we still visit with his lovely wife, Alicia, also a medical doctor.

CHAPTER 10

HUNGER

No one who has not truly suffered from hunger can ever hope to understand fully what it entails.
The German occupation of the Eastern territories of Europe was not only cruel, but it was cleverly designed to differentiate between the different types of people; and one of the methods was the degree of starvation and or supply of food. In the concentration camps, those in charge simply allowed people to starve to death. In the forced labor camps, they fed them enough only to prolong their suffering to a degree, and let them die afterwards, because they could not ever let them get out -- as for instance in the super secret rocket factories operated in underground tunnels.
Then there was the question of the Polish people. Although they produced a large amount of food, which was shipped to Germany, they themselves were kept on the brink of starvation. Russian prisoners of war were starved to death by the hundreds of thousands. The German administration was unable to provide for the upkeep of several million war prisoners who came suddenly into their hands. Naturally, the Germans did not care a bit!

And where was the "International Committee of the Red Cross?" NOWHERE!

The Red Cross was totally inactive in the great sufferings of the War in Eastern Europe. I could only detect Red Cross activities that were run by the German Army and the German Red Cross. In fact I observed some Red Cross prisoner of war packages in the German Soldatenheim (soldier's home) and other places. I saw thousands of Russian prisoners of war in deplorable condition -- starved, emaciated, in rags -- being marched along the roads. I could not identify a trace of the Red Cross in the concentration camps of Belzec, Janowska, or Ebensee in Austria. These were the camps I saw with my own eyes. The Red Cross has an abominable record of inactivity during these horrific times.

During the late fall and early winter of 1941/42, I was in a building work gang for a Polish building firm, which in turn had building contracts for German Military Proving Grounds. They constructed artillery ranges and tank exercise terrain, access roads, as well as barracks. The work gangs consisted of 6 - 8 workers, who were trucked out every morning to their various building sites by a foreman who told them roughly what to do. They were left alone to work until around noon, when a kettle of soup was brought out with a piece of bread for everyone. The foreman returned with the truck around 6:00 P.M. and took the workers back to the office. The productivity of the half-starved workers was almost nil. The foremen understood that, so did the firm and everyone else -- EXCEPT the Germans. They proclaimed that the "Damned Poles" were just lazy!

    To ask for food was not only an exercise in futility, but extremely unwise, even dangerous. We were issued food stamps, which had to be brought to the office of the firm, and there they cut off most of the coupons for the little noon meal that they provided. With the remaining coupons we had to go to a grocery store to get whatever you could. Very few of the coupons could be redeemed because of the lack of food available.

    Naturally, there was also a black market, but with the wages we were paid there was little possibility of obtaining food from black market sources. I still have these food stamps today -- as an historical curiosity!

    One of my happiest recollections from this bleak time was finding fields of harvested potatoes, some of which had remained. In the morning we went immediately to collect the overlooked potatoes. We buried them in a hole, covered them with earth, and built a fire over them. Later we had a fine meal of baked potatoes -- a great treat! In winter the potatoes were frozen and had a sweet taste, though a strongly nauseating effect.

The German administration living in the "General Government" lived like KINGS! It was obvious, however, that most of these people came from rather small time, low income surroundings in Germany, and lived in opulence and luxury unknown to them previously. After that came the German military, which was supplied and fed rather adequately. In the beginning of the occupation, the Ukrainians were cooperative with the Germans and lived a lot better than the Poles. But that did not last too long. German policies were so restrictive and so unwise and crude that they very shortly alienated the Ukrainians, who then began supporting the underground.

With acts of terrorism by the Ukrainian (Soviet) Partisans against the German military, the German administration turned viciously against the Ukrainians as much as against the Poles. Black marketing was also severely punished, usually by transferring offenders to the K. Z. (concentration camps).

At the bottom of the ladder, of course, were the Jews. They were just plainly hunted and killed.

CHAPTER 11

LWOW UNDER THE NAZIS
THE GHETTO

The events from 1939 to 1945 were so overwhelming and also fast-moving that it is difficult sometimes to distinguish between what happened at a certain time of year, such as, for instance, spring of 1941, or '42, or '43. Consequently, some of my recollections might be off one way or the other.

It is also very difficult now that over fifty years have passed, to recall exactly the sequence of events, though the events themselves are not apt to be eradicated from my mind. In fact, my life is punctuated consistently, almost every day, with thoughts and feelings that are connected with these times.

On the 29th of June 1941 the bombardment of Lwow started and the following day German Army troops entered the city on bicycles. A Ukrainian S.S. Death Head division named "Nachtigal" accompanied them also. They were trained and recruited previously in Germany, and represented the ultra nationalist parties of the Ukrainians. Within the last few days the Red Army left Lwow. Very few civilians were allowed to leave. The Soviets did not want to let civilians follow them east. The considerations of the Soviets were always of political nature. Most likely they did not want to have spies or opponents move into the eastern territories and then organize resistance against their administration and army.

During that time there was quite a bit of looting, particularly the Soviet government stores of food. There was a whole week of anarchy. My family and most of the middle class and Jewish population did not go out on the streets

As the German and Ukrainian troops moved toward the center of the city, the Ukrainian population enthusiastically greeted them, and a great number of flowers were given to them and thrown onto the marching soldiers. Since I was also on the streets at that time, I could observe that most of the greeting population was Ukrainians, but there were also a certain percentage of Poles.

Virtually all Ukrainians and Poles hated the Soviet regime, although the Poles had an equal antipathy toward the Germans who had defeated them and occupied their country. The only ones who were relatively satisfied with the Soviet occupation were the Jewish population, since the Soviet administration represented a certain amount of protection against the murderous Germans.

Quickly after the entry of the first German troops, there was the rumor going around that the Soviets had murdered all the prisoners in the city prisons. It must be assumed that some of their political prisoners were probably executed. However, the so-called "prison action," which took place afterwards, was reported by the Germans as being spontaneous. Nothing could be more untrue. A large number of well-organized people descended upon the city and started to kill mostly Jews, and this Pogrom started the end of June and lasted for four days. On the basis of post-War research, within this period of time approximately 7,000 Jews were killed outright on the streets of Lwow. The streets, especially in the inner city, were covered with dead bodies that had been either shot or their heads bashed in with stones or wooden bats. Many hundreds were put on trucks and carried out to some of the suburbs of Lwow and liquidated there. The Germans had the Ukrainians drag the Jews out of their houses and their basements and the various places where they tried to hide. They were forced to lay face down out on the streets. Thereafter the German military, as well as the Ukrainian police went around and shot them with sub-machine guns.

    Shortly after the occupation the local newspapers started up both in Ukrainian and Polish, and they described these events as a natural result of the hatred created by the Soviet departure and their crimes. From then on, almost on a daily basis new sanctions, persecutions, and harassment of the Jews occurred. All these actions were greeted in general with great satisfaction by both the Ukrainian and the Polish population.

First of all any kind of travel by train was forbidden to Jews. They were allowed for a while to use the last car on the local tram, but only standing up. Then this too was totally prohibited. There was also a curfew that started at 8:00 P.M., which was difficult for those people who worked late hours. The coupons distributed among the population entitling the purchase of bread and other foodstuffs were restricted severely for the Jewish population. They got a lot less to eat than the rest.

The Germans made constant arrests during the night by. Although at the time it was not known, they used the Lwow telephone book to find Jewish sounding names and then arrested these people, since the telephones were normally owned by middle class or higher educated Jews.

All Jewish people had to register and report to the "Arbeitsamt" or work agency, which was created in August 1941. Various German organizations or businesses picked them up to do the work. For this work they were never paid, and only in a few instances were they given extra food.

As young as I was I had enough good sense to suspect any and all German administrative offices, and I never went to the Arbeitsamt. I circumvented that by finding myself a job and having that business register me at the Arbeitsamt and supply me with the necessary documentation. This system kept me out of their range. It was very smart because it turned out that any surplus labor that was around was shipped away to so-called "work camps." As it turned out, most of these work camps were either concentration camps or annihilation camps, and the people shipped out never came back.

    For some reason all these aspects had a way of traveling back to the population rather fast. There was always someone who managed to escape and told the story.

    At that time the consolidation of the Jewish population of Lwow into a ghetto had not yet taken place. The way the German administration worked it; they declared certain parts of the city as "Judenrein" (cleaned of Jews), so that Jews living in those parts had to move to other areas within 24 hours. This system continued until September 1942 when they had all the Jewish population concentrated into a very small area where they could easily be governed and compressed, then eventually transported away to the concentration and annihilation camps.

    During the various stages of our residence in Lwow we lived in diverse locations. We finally wound up in the ghetto of Lwow. Good work papers issued by a German authority sometimes prevented sudden arrest and deportation. Naturally with the Jewish Star of David arm-band, you were really not fully protected by anything. Daily executions took place, not only in the prisons but also on the streets. Summary executions were perpetrated mostly by German or Ukrainian "S.S." men. However, it did not take long for me to figure out that, even being a Jew, if I had good working papers I would be less likely to be arrested and "shipped out." Moreover, it was best not to be a Jew at all.

    So I started operating by going to work without the arm-band, which, of course, was punishable by immediate execution. I would leave the ghetto with my arm-band, show my work papers at the gate, and then on my way to work, dodge into a house that had entrances on both sides. I would remove my blue star armband and put it into my pocket, and then walk out the other side as a non-Jew, so to speak. This enabled me to use the streetcars, which were forbidden to Jews. It also protected me from street patrols and all kinds of other harassment.

    I had a job for a short while as a clean-up boy in a German military barracks. They did not pay me with money but with some army provisions. This was fine with me because with the working papers from the German barracks, I could carry this food home.

While I worked there I became acquainted with a young German soldier who was about my own age, and we became quite friendly. Whenever they sent details into the countryside to pick up wood or other supplies on the truck, he would ask his sergeant if he could take one of the local helpers along -- me. They took me along on their trucks to nearby villages to help load and unload, which enabled me to give rides to local farmers, who wanted to come into the city. These people usually gave me tips in form of a little piece of butter or some bread, or some other foodstuff, which I took home. This enabled us to avoid outright famine in our little family. These little trips also provided a certain amount of variety.

My parents, of course, were at home and there wasn't too much for them to do. My mother did not speak Polish or Ukrainian, so she was virtually unemployable; and my father was not very well, so their circumstances were quite precarious.

Almost every night we gathered in the apartment of one of our neighbors, Mr. Lichtenstein. He had an excellent short wave radio, a Telefunken. I was dispatched into a very small bedroom, where I hovered over the radio with a heavy blanket over my head and the radio so no one could possibly overhear what I was listening to -- the daily newscast of the BBC (British Broadcasting Corporation). Since I was the only one who spoke and understood English, it was my duty to listen to this, (making no notes), and then come back into the main room and explain what I had heard to the little group of my parents and their close friends. I heard the speeches of Roosevelt and Churchill. Listening to "enemy broadcasts" such as the BBC or Voice of America was a capital offense. In the years of 1938 and 39, prior to the outbreak of the War, I listened to the radio a lot. But it wasn't the BBC I listened to, it was always Radio Moscow. Radio Moscow was the only radio station that broadcast in many languages very critical and combative broadcasts directed against the Nazi government of Germany. No American, English, French or even Polish station would do anywhere near such a thing. The Democracies at that time seemed to be paralyzed and unwilling and unable to counter the onslaught of the German propaganda machine. It was only Moscow that countered it, and countered it well.

It was a great shock to me, when during our escape from Warsaw; half of Poland was occupied by the Soviets and the other half by the Germans according to a secret, undercover pact between

Nazi Germany and the Soviet Union. The treachery and falsehood of the Soviets came to light to me with an exceptional kind of clarity. It was then and there that I understood how devious and immoral were any and all totalitarian regimes, to be held in total contempt.

Not long thereafter, my German Soldier friend's unit moved toward the Eastern Front, and my whole employment scheme at this barracks became very shaky. (Most German soldiers were afraid of the "East" as the Eastern Front was considered a punishment and a death sentence. My friendly soldier told me time and again that his parents prayed that he would be spared from having to fight on the Eastern Front.

When the German military post was transferred further to the Eastern Front, I lost my employment. I frantically looked for another place where I could get work.

It was crucial to have good work papers, and fast.... Legally I was obliged to report to the Arbeitsamt within 24 hours. This was quite dangerous because they could stick you anywhere -- particularly into some of the jobs where we knew we would not come out alive. These jobs, connected with war production, were bestowed not only upon Jews, but also upon Poles and other less desirable nationalities, which were stuck into underground factories and just plainly worked to death. This was known! Whenever there were round-ups (so called "Lapanka") we did not know if they were looking for young men, old people, or women.

Not far from downtown Lwow there was a beautiful little park, at the center of which was a Renaissance villa. It looked somewhat like the pictures of the little aristocratic hunting lodges or like "Sans Souci." On it was fixed a brand new large shield with the Red Cross at both ends and in big letters, "Soldaten Heim." It was a way-station for German soldiers, somewhat resembling the American USO. It was run by Red Cross nurses called "Sisters." I walked in the rear door with my Jewish arm band on, and asked whether I could see someone to obtain work. The young nurse made me wait and back came an older woman in her starched nurse's cap, with a Red Cross prominently displayed in front, and a white uniform. Since I spoke somewhat "broken German," I was hired on the spot.

They needed workers to carry up coal from the basement, tend the furnaces, and do a lot of yard work. I was told immediately that there would be no pay, but I would get all I could eat. I asked if I could be given a work pass certifying my employment, otherwise I could not come to work. I got this document.

The next day I was to report at 7:00 A.M. The elder Red Cross sisters turned out to be old line Nazis, wearing their Nazi Party insignias on their Red Cross uniforms. The head sister was Sister Erma. Of the several Jewish unpaid slave workers, there was also a young boy of approximately 12 years called Frederick. He obviously came from a good family, and was not used to physical labor. I helped him along somewhat, since I was fortunate enough at that time to be in good, strong condition.

Then a curious thing happened. His father brought him to work in the morning. A university professor, distinguished looking with gray hair and mustache, he started spending considerable time in the office with Sister Erma. All these meetings took place early in the morning. Through various small remarks made by young Frederick, I came to the realization that the super-Nazi Red Cross head sister of the Soldaten Heim was accepting considerable bribes to ship young Frederick somewhere and somehow save him. His father had correctly assessed the situation. Sure enough, a couple of weeks later, young Frederick simply disappeared.

Not long after that, the entire Jewish detail of the Soldaten Heim was fired. We were told that Sister Erma did not want to have any Jews around the Soldaten Heim. Now the search to quickly find another job and work papers started again.

Toward the section where we used to live before the war, I found that one of the side streets bore a military sign showing that this was an Italian military command of the eastern front. This was in a four story building, which was previously a school. I didn't speak a word of Italian, but I did have six years of Latin instruction, and consequently I felt that perhaps I could somehow communicate with the people. And so I did!

It was a small Italian way-station in Lwow where their various couriers, officers, and also enlisted men would be fed and refitted or could stay over night until the next train was available to take them to their deployment at the eastern front. Although I did not know it at the time, and neither did they: the Italian units that were committed to the eastern front by Mussolini to help his friend from the north, Adolph Hitler, would be completely annihilated in the battles of Stalingrad and others, and there were hardly any survivors who got back home to Italy.

They hired me as a kitchen helper. This was an ideal position because I was near food, and food was all important.

"Buongiorno, Capitano!" **Don't** call me "Capitano," he yelled for the 4th or 5th time when

I greeted the head of the kitchen, Sergeant Luigi Del Fabbro. "Call me Sergeant Luigi, I've told you a million times." He laughed and told me to clean out the various kettles that were left from the previous meal.

The kettles were about 4 foot in diameter and 3 feet deep. There were three of them, and they needed to be cleaned out so that he could cook up a huge amount of pasta for the next meal.

The job at the Italian command was one of the best things that I ran into during the whole war. They did not treat us as Jews or non-Jews. They just asked us to do some jobs, and they were very polite; and best of all I was able to take home a large jug of leftovers of macaroni or soup, or whatever I could scrounge to my parents every evening. At that time we did not yet live in the ghetto, but a little bit outside, where we had a very small room. That large jug of food was very welcome, and we all lived off the remnants of the Italian kitchen.

The Lwow station was commanded by a Lieutenant who demonstratively showed what a good Fascist he was by often times clicking his heels and raising his hand in the Fascist salute, and always having German officers as guests. The conditions at the Italian military station were very pleasant. Several Jewish girls worked there as chamber maids and clean-up crews. I observed this

Italian Lieutenant in a love affair with a Jewish girl who worked with us. She confided to me that she hoped he might help to get her out of Poland and save her. The situation was sometimes almost comical; and we all snickered and laughed a lot about some of our observations. I never knew whether or not the Lieutenant saved the girl eventually, but he was her one hope of getting out of those terrible conditions.

    I worked at the Italian military kitchen for a couple of months, up to the time I escaped from the Lwow ghetto with my friend Janek to Rawa Ruska.

    A couple of years later at Buia/Osoppo, a construction site in Northern Italy only a few kilometers away from Udine there occurred a tremendous coincidence, hard to believe! By that time with false papers I had become "Tadeusz Chwistek," a Polish assistant to the manager of the road building firm. We went into Udine many times, either to eat at a restaurant or go shopping. On a very bright sunny morning walking down the main street of Udine I heard someone yelling "Enrico!" It was my cook, Luigi del Fabbro, who in the meantime was lucky enough to be decommissioned.

    As his helper I was known as "Enrico" which was the nearest thing to my first name, Heinz. But in Udine I was known as Theo

Chwistek. Aside from this dangerous mix-up, I was overwhelmed to meet this wonderful, nice, well-meaning Italian boy. Most Italians I met during the war were so much more sympathetic and kind in comparison to some of their northern neighbors. We met on several occasions in Udine and in the environs. His wife's best friend married a member of the Polish army and moved to Poland after the war. Luigi's wife told me that her husband became abusive and violent when he drank a lot. I lost track of Luigi del Fabbro and I heard that he was hospitalized because of his alcoholism, and eventually died because of it.

There was another interesting and frightful adventure. Often times I was sent from Buia to the nearby railway station in Gemona to pick up supplies, parcels or mail for Firma Stickel. Usually I went with a truck driver. On one occasion, shortly after siesta around 3:00 P.M. in the afternoon, we drove up to the train station in Gemona to pick up several parcels and packs of mail. We put it all next to me in the truck and drove off to Buia.

Going over the railway tracks, we slowed down, and at that moment two young men in civilian clothes jumped on the running board of the truck on both sides. One stranger pulled out a pistol and started shooting! He got off about four shots before I had enough presence of mind to open the door of the truck and knock him off, as the driver did the same to the man on his side. All the shots crossed in front of my belly and the steering wheel of the truck driver. Except for a few scratches from the shattered glass of the truck window, neither one of us was hurt. The driver stepped on the gas and drove off with great speed to get away from the whole scene. It turned out that this was an attack by the partisans, who did not know of my connection and my cooperation with them. Such are the winds of war.

CHAPTER 12

JANEK
ESCAPE FROM THE GHETTO

Within one day after invading the Soviet Union the Germans swept into Lwow. The Red Army withdrew as fast as they possibly could in disorganized flight - a rout. The Ukrainians and some Poles greeted the Nazi invaders as liberators from Communist oppression. The German Army troops were greeted enthusiastically on the main roads with flowers. Many Ukrainians appeared with armbands in the colors of the Ukrainian movement, and a local puppet government was installed, as well as an exclusively Ukrainian police force.

The Soviet authorities, milicja (police), army M.Ps., and NKVD forces prevented the escape of almost all civilians toward the east. The Soviets feared that many Nazi collaborators and spies would move with them and cause considerable damage to their military operations.

The Germans had found a strong ally among the Ukrainian population. But in Nazi "German Master Race" philosophy, all Slavic peoples, such as Ukrainians, Poles, and Russians were "Untermenschen" – Sub-humans. Hitler ordered a ruthless and cruel campaign against these people.

Over a period of a year, the Germans managed to alienate the local population by their undiplomatic and savage governance, so that their original good will turned into hatred. As conditions became more intolerable, with the lack of food and other supplies, the executions of actual and perceived opponents, a large influx of Ukrainian, Polish, and Jewish men joined the partisans. They in turn were controlled by the Soviets and became an important part of the War behind the front lines. The dynamiting of train tracks, troop trains, the poisoning of wells, and the shooting of German soldiers became commonplace.

As soon as the Germans moved in they announced many new and constantly changing orders, directed against the Ukrainians, Poles, Jews, and gypsies. These orders, in German, Ukrainian and Polish, were affixed to buildings and announcement columns all over the city. Non-compliance was punishable by death. There was a death penalty for virtually everything in contravention to the German occupation rules.

In the process of new orders, my small family (my father, Jakob (Kuba), my mother, Frieda, and I) moved into four different places within a few months. Wherever we moved, a few weeks thereafter that part of the city had to be "Juderein" (clean of Jews), and we had to move again. We started in a little apartment, then a nice room rented to us by a Polish family, and from there we moved into a wee, tiny room on the south side of the city. Finally, we too were forced into the walls of the Ghetto, where we were assigned sleeping places on an asphalt floor in a large dirty empty factory.

The factory had small, grimy windows, which let in the light, but when the sun shone, there was no shade. People pasted bits of paper over the windows to avoid the sun. It was communal living with absolutely no privacy. The unhappiness of my poor mother is hard to describe. The change from our luxurious apartment in Warsaw to these miserable surroundings left her, at times, in a daze. No one could have adjusted happily to these living conditions, but she took it hardest of all of us.

In this large hall we were forced to call "home," our assigned sleeping quarters were close to those of Janek's parents, who were thrown into the Lwow Ghetto at the same time that we were. Janek was 17 years old, and I was a bit older. Though we had gone to school together, we didn't know one another well, for he was in another class. He was a quiet, rather good looking young chap with a tanned face, black, short hair, and almond shaped eyes. As I got to know him better I realized that he had integrity and a superb character, which belied his age. It was this quietly determined young man who helped me take my first, critical steps on the precarious pathway out of the Holocaust. Yet he soon slipped on this perilous path and instantly disappeared. His tragedy was my first close call with death. It was a crisis for which I was not prepared, and yet I had to handle it on my own.

Because I was working in the Italian Expeditionary Army kitchens seven days a week, and was out early and came back late, I didn't see much of him. Janek had gotten some "Aryan" papers and found employment with a Polish building firm that had contracts to do work on the German tank proving grounds in Rawa Ruska. He came to visit his parents on weekends, and there was ample time for our parents to talk between themselves. He told them that if I could come up with some "Aryan" papers -- birth certificate and "Abmeldung" (a registered "move" authority from the German administration showing you had permission to leave one place to go to another) he could get me a job with the Polish building firm, Stronski in Rawa Ruska, a small provincial town about 50 miles from Lwow.

As soon as my family wound up in the Ghetto factory, we talked over our sad situation. My mother cried a lot. She was dejected and full of terrible foreboding. As it turned out, her feelings were very accurate. My father and I discussed the various possibilities and we came to the abysmal conclusion that it would be best for me to get out of the Ghetto. On the outside, perhaps, I could be more helpful to my parents.

We did not know exactly what the real dangers were at that time. We did not know how and where annihilation took place, but we did know that there were terrible slave labor camps, beatings, shootings and persecutions. The Germans were already shrinking the Lwow Ghetto, and young people seemed the most vulnerable. As we talked and discussed our plight, my mother, of course, was appalled at the idea of our small family splitting up and of losing her only son. My father felt it was the only sensible and realistic thing to do -- to part ways and to try to establish at least me on the outside.

In retrospect, I think that he had a pretty good idea that we would probably be parting forever. In fact, after I left the Ghetto I never saw my mother again, and my father only twice. Although I didn't realize it at the time, he most likely was trying to save my life. And in fact, he did!

So my father and Janek's parents hatched a plan. My father somehow bought me papers -- consisting of three documents -- on the black market for some $20.00 (U.S. dollar bills). One was a birth certificate from a Catholic parish, probably genuine, under the name of Tadeusz Chwistek. Another stated that I had been working under that name for an electrical firm in Lwow. The third was a blank "out - registration" form, obviously stolen from the city administration -- proof that the bearer was permitted to leave his previous residence and move to another. I smiled as I filled out this form! The Germans had such great confidence in their bureaucratic system to monitor the movements of the population in the occupied areas. I used a phony address and signed it with the name of a former landlord. These documents, good as they were, had one common flaw: they were without photos. The solution, according to Janek, was with my new employer. "You give the papers to Stronski personnel office and they will run to the Arbeitsamt (German labor office) themselves and arrange everything for you. They are building some training grounds for tanks on a contract from the German Army! They are always short of labor and have a lot of dirt to move. Stronski would hate to see the Germans assign you to another firm. Just ask them to issue you a new identity card with a photo.... "

    Subsequently I applied for food stamps under this new name. Much later I obtained a driver's license. With painstaking care I deliberately went from office to organization to association and built myself a dossier. With these false papers I lived and worked for over 4 years, until the end of World War II.

One dark evening in October Janek came to Lwow for me as promised. It was a tearful good-by with my parents, and very short. Janek was standing nearby urging, "Come on, hurry up, our train will be leaving shortly." I didn't wish to prolong this difficult parting, so I just kissed them good-by, turned on my heel, and departed with Janek. My mother cried and wailed, "We'll never see you again." My father was also very distressed, but there was a glimmer of hope in his eyes. I also was optimistic, thinking that if we could somehow survive these dreadful times we would find each other again and start out where we had left off. Then a dark premonition came over me on hearing my mother's tearful remarks. Unfortunately, she was right, and I never saw her again, although I saw my father twice afterwards, but as an emaciated prisoner in a concentration camp, and near death.

Janek always spoke to me quietly, twisting his lips and speaking to me from the corner of his mouth. This was one of his psychological defenses as he tried to emphasize the necessity for secrecy and the need to keep away from other people. Among other things, he said, "Make sure you sleep or pretend to sleep in the railway car. We do not want to have any kind of conversation with anyone."

In the darkness we climbed the wall of the Ghetto where the wall was damaged, ran across a dark alley, around a corner and into one of the houses that had entrances on both sides of the building. We threw away our blue and white "Star of David" armbands on our way to the Lwow railway station to catch the night train to Rawa Ruska. In the dirty little compartment, Janek sat close to me, and with lowered voice, gave me a detailed account of our situation and explained what to do next.

As we slipped out of the Ghetto that cold evening in the late fall of 1941, Janek wore an inconspicuous navy blue coat and a dark knit cap. I carried a small package with few belongings -- a shirt or two, a couple of pairs of socks and underwear, a comb and a few toiletries. My mother wanted me to take more, but I refused. I realized that we were about to start living on the edge of a knife, two Jewish teenagers with false identity papers hiding in Rawa Ruska. I feared that my parents would need those personal provisions even more than I. With my departure, they lost their breadwinner.

There was lots of snow, turning to slush, and adequate footwear was almost unobtainable for civilians in Nazi occupied Eastern Poland. Those forced to work in the mud and slush without good footwear were indeed miserable. Because I knew I would be working outdoors, I had bartered for a pair of heavy leather farmers boots, high and sturdy.   Late that night as we arrived in Rawa Ruska and trudged through the darkness to Janek's place, the town seemed very little. A small stream ran through the middle with a road and tiny houses squatting on either side. The so-called "downtown" section had a market place and a small Ghetto.

There was a curfew, of course, but in case a patrol stopped us Janek was prepared with special permission for workers for the military administration. We reached a peasant cottage, knocked, and were let in. "This is my friend who is going to share my room with me," Janek told the Ukrainian landlady. "I already told you about him." She said, "Fine! Goodnight!" And that was it.

Janek's room was the only bedroom in the house. It was clean and had two small beds. The Ukrainian woman's husband, a conscript in the Polish Army, had been missing in action since September of 1939. She lived with her small daughter in the kitchen area near the stove. The "house" consisted of the kitchen and our one little room. There was no heat, no running water and an outdoor toilet. She and her child lived off the rent, plus keeping a few chickens in the "back yard."

Our rent was relatively low, but I don't remember in which currency it was paid. Currencies changed so fast during the War: first we had Polish Zlotys. Then came the Soviets and we had freshly printed Rubles. Then, all of a sudden, we had German Occupation Marks. Then Zlotys again. Then Reichsmarks, which were illegal for non-Germans to possess. Also in circulation were green U.S. Dollars, the most sought after and respected currency, though illegal and subject to confiscation and prison.

The following morning at about 6:30 we crossed the creek on some boards; and in a house on a sandy country road found the offices of the Stronski firm, owned by a Polish engineer from Warsaw. We walked in and saw a supervisor and a secretary bent over a typewriter.

Janek was well organized, and it was obvious that he had already prepared the terrain. He said, "This is Chwistek. If you want him, he has his papers." The Supervisor said, "Yes, we'll take him!" I immediately asked them to get my identity documents with photos so I could visit friends and family in Lwow. I "just happened" to have passport photos with me, filled in the necessary forms, and they issued me a statement on their letterhead saying that I was employed by the Stronski firm. A couple of weeks later I was given a genuine identity paper with my photo -- a most valuable document that helped me create many others. I also managed to get back my false "out-registration" (Abmeldung) statement under the pretext that I needed it for some other police registration. It was the weakest of my papers and not one I wanted to float around in a Stronski file.

During the months I worked for Stronski I worked to adapt myself to my new identity. I drilled myself, "I am Tadeusz Chwistek Tadeusz Chwistek Tadeusz Chwistek Tadeusz Chwistek" with my supposed parents names, my false birth date, etc. I worried that I might talk in my sleep while dreaming or that someone might wake me abruptly and I might give myself away. I positively could not afford to. I developed new personal habits. I stopped memorizing people's last names. It was important NOT to know those names. They often were not real and changed frequently. Any confusion would be dangerous. In Lwow I had heard the name of Janek's parents; but in Rawa Ruska I made a conscious effort to forget it and remember only the name on his Aryan papers. I can recall neither now.

I began my "career" at Stronski as a common laborer. I didn't have any skills to speak of. They got me a shovel and a pick, and I learned to use them, building roads as long as the weather held. Later on I became certified as a "road technician," which made my life a lot easier.

Janek was assigned to another labor gang, so we seldom saw one another during the day. During the evenings we talked a lot, exchanging bits of information and experiences, and trying to prop up one another's spirits. We both worried about our parents and felt lonely. We could both sense that tragedy was looming on the horizon and dreamed and schemed about how we were going to smuggle our parents out of the Ghetto to the partisans. It was an absolute impossibility, of course, but it helped to scheme. The partisans didn't want older people, especially Jews.

Janek disappeared approximately 6 weeks after he brought me to Rawa Ruska. One evening he did not come home to our little cottage. I thought that perhaps he had stayed late with friends or with a girl. I put out our kerosene lamp and climbed into bed, figuring that when he came, he would surely wake me up.

But in the morning Janek wasn't there. He had never missed a night's sleep in his bed before. As I went through the kitchen on my way to work, the landlady, an uneasy expression on her face, handed me a white postcard. The text was in Ukrainian, but it was signed "Geheime Staats Polizei" -- **GESTAPO**: the dreaded German Secret Police, notorious for its cunning and cruelty. I was summoned to appear at their headquarters in Rawa

Ruska in room 238 between 10:00 and 12 noon the next day.

    I realized then what had happened. Janek had been snared as a hiding Jew, and they wanted to interview me as his roommate. Did they know that I was hiding as well? The landlady confirmed that two men in uniform had come the previous evening and forced Janek to go with them. He had either been denounced or made some mistake that had helped the Germans to track him down.

    I tucked the postcard into my pocket and went out to think things over. It occurred to me that if the Gestapo suspected I was a hiding Jew, they wouldn't have bothered to leave a postcard, but would have posted a sentry or agent to arrest me. They had so many volunteer police employees around town that it would have been no problem for them to set a trap for me. I reasoned that the Gestapo was merely checking.

    The next question I had to ponder was whether to run? If I ran, my papers would be compromised – worthless. My false name would go on the "wanted" list. I didn't have money to buy new documents or the necessary contacts to go through the rigmarole of re-establishing myself with a new identity. I soon concluded that I would have to go to the Gestapo, and just play as dumb as I could.

I went to my firm and told them I could not work that morning because I had an appointment to register with the police. I didn't tell them it was the Gestapo. That would have frightened them or made them suspicious of me.

I found the Gestapo offices in a two-storied, gray building that looked to me about a mile long, fifteen minutes ahead of time for my "interrogation." The building was also the German Army administration of the proving grounds. I walked a long corridor until I found a gray door with a little shield marked with black digits "238." Will I ever forget it?

I waited outside in the corridor a good half hour before I knocked. Someone shouted, "Herein!" (Enter!) I stepped inside, cap in hand. A low ranking S.S. man at a desk didn't bother to look up, so I stood there until he deigned to address me. He studied my postcard and motioned me to the next room where another man, clad in a light green uniform with the black "death's head" insignia sat at his desk.

Knowing the German character, disposition, instincts, and prejudices, I kept a ramrod straight **posture, my hands stiffly at my sides,** and I spoke as a recruit would to his sergeant. Beside the German Gestapo man at a smaller table was a Ukrainian in a non-descript German army uniform. He acted as a translator and spoke Polish with me.

After routine questions about my name, birthplace, address, employment and so forth, he asked me whether I knew a fellow by the name of Janek X. "Of course I know him! He's my roommate," I answered. "What do you know about him," he snapped. "Not much," I replied. "He comes from Lwow, at least that is where his family comes from." I explained that Firma Stronski had advised me about the possibility of sharing room rent with another worker, and had put me in touch with him. I had shared a room with him for only a few weeks, and we hardly saw one another, since we worked on different crews. All this time I tried to keep a sincere, dull expression on my face. In the midst of the interrogation, however, I cheekily demanded to know what had happened to him, why he had been taken away and when he would be coming back. "I need him to pay his half of the rent. Is he going to come back and pay his share? Or do I have to go out and find someone to pay half? I can't afford to pay it all myself." I kept this whining and complaining up for quite a long time.

      The Gestapo man was at first stupefied, and then infuriated at my self-absorption and imbecility. Rising in a rage from behind his desk, he screamed **"RAUS!!"** and motioned for me to get the hell out of his office. I hastened to obey! I suppose I was the only Jew ever to be thrown out of a Gestapo interrogation instead of being arrested.

    I never saw or heard from Janek again.

CHAPTER 13

TERROR

How can I express the Nazi system of intimidation and terror to an average American citizen who has never been forced to live under such demoralizing conditions? The unrelenting dread, fear and the grim life that one led under the Nazi terror system are difficult to depict in their full horror.

It was the Nazis deliberate policy to sustain fear in everyone at all times. As I traveled through Germany and Austria, people were afraid to talk to strangers and also suspicious of friends, because the Nazi party apparatus utilized denunciation as a tool. A child might report on his parents; so the parents had to be very careful about what they said in front of their children, who might repeat it in school in front of a party member. Then a case could be made against the parents or brothers or sisters or acquaintances.

The constant threat of being committed to the degradation, depredations, and horrible death of a concentration camp was ever present. The intimidation was so thorough, that even among the Nazi cadres there was constant suspicion and fright. One might be ratting on the other. In the workplaces the same system prevailed. People would denounce others in order to advance to a better job.

However, this was nothing compared to what transpired as one moved further east. Once you moved into the territories of former Poland, or Russia, or the Ukraine, the picture changed rapidly for the worse. The taking of hostages was commonplace. You constantly either witnessed or heard about summary executions. Traveling through the various parts of Poland or the Ukraine, it was not uncommon to see dead bodies shot beside the road, beside the railway tracks or against a wall. I often saw people hanging from ropes with signs pinned to them indicating that they were partisans, or that they had shot at a German soldier.

In the eastern territories, various levels of intimidation and fright existed at all strata of society. The local population was at the very bottom. Any German, whether he was civilian or in uniform could take out a gun and shoot and kill a local citizen without any fear of arrest or retribution. It was often done.

Above the civilians were the local police, under the direction of some German sergeant of the police, above the local commander, who told them what to do or not to do. When it came to the Germans themselves, there were again strata. The regular army, soldiers or officers were both suspicious and afraid of the S. S. officers, because the S. S. operated totally outside the realm of military command or discipline. Even among the S. S. there was a certain amount of apprehension, because on top of them all were two organizations that had the right of life and death over anyone: the Gestapo, (Geheime Staats Polizei), which meant Secret State Police; and the S. D. (Sicherheits Dienst or Security Service). These were special units that operated under direct command of the Sicherheitshauptamt (Main Security Office), which was headed by Heinrich Himmler in Berlin. Members of both organizations could appear either in uniform or civilian clothes. They had right of entry everywhere, and took actions outside of any kind of control.

  As the war progressed, I moved from the eastern territories into Italy. There the situation was at first somewhat different. The German command was subject to Italian administration and laws. Consequently, if the Germans wanted to mount an action against the partisans, they first coordinated that with the Italian military. My impression was that the Italian command structure was reluctant and unwilling to join with German forces in retaliatory actions against their own civilians. Consequently, things were a lot more civil in Italy than they were either in Germany or the eastern territories.

All this changed during the War, as the Italian government fell and the southern part of Italy joined the Allies. The northern part became the so-called "Social Republic of Italy" with a temporary capital in Salo on Lake Garda. Then there was absolutely no holding back the Germans. The northern part of Italy became a German occupied territory and the Germans performed their nefarious actions with no regard to Italian administration at all. Oftentimes villages were surrounded and hostages were taken, because of either actual or perceived attacks upon Germans.

The Italian underground and partisan organizations were strong and active. But there was always terrible uncertainty and argument about tactics we should follow. The result of any successful action against the Germans provoked a horrendous, murderous retaliation and killing of civilian hostages. We were constantly torn between decisions that might result in the annihilation of innocent people. Nevertheless, we could not abandon the fight against the occupying Germans. This dilemma was common to all the resistance movements throughout Europe, whether in France or Holland, Poland, Ukraine or Russia.

The Italian underground organizations were widespread and, to the best of my knowledge, not centrally directed. I found out at the end of the War that there were all kinds of competing groups devoted to different ideologies; but in the area where we operated the centers were in the Italian towns of Tarcento, Pontebba, Gemona, and other areas to the south and east.

During one of our actions we were able to lure a whole company of German soldiers into the hills above Tarcento. They simply disappeared! There was never any further trace of them. After the disappearance of the German company above Tarcento there was no retaliation. If we made the Germans disappear and there were no witnesses, there was no one against whom to retaliate. This action decidedly confused and rattled the Germans, which made us decide that any such further opportunity would be worthwhile pursuing. However, this was the only instance I can remember where we were able to achieve this goal. It gave us great satisfaction to spread some terror ourselves, for a change. I have no idea what actually happened to this German company that disappeared in the hills above Tarcento. I imagine they were all killed.

I recall vividly the tremendous fear the Germans had of being captured by the Partisans in the eastern parts, because the Partisans had no facilities to keep prisoners. The Soviets directed their Partisans to immediately shoot any Germans captured.

It was remarkable to me that as soon as the War ended, there were so many Austrian resistance fighters with Red/White/Red armbands to be seen running prominently hither and yon. During the War, I could not detect the slightest amount of any such activity, or even any talk about any kind of resistance in Austria. If it did exist it was minimal and did not come to my attention.

Outside of the mass murders in the various eastern villages of Rawa Ruska, Luck, Simferopol, etc. the greatest amount of terror to which I was witness was in the city of Lvov. Executions every few days were commonplace, and they were publicized! It was the policy of the occupiers to discourage any kind of resistance by intimidation, no matter what the provocation might have been.

During my passage through the Ukraine on one of my trips, suddenly there was a lot of commotion in a small Ukrainian village. The local Ukrainian police as well as virtually all German Army officers were ordered to go to the little market place in the center of this village. There lined up against the wall of a house were six or seven persons, two of them women. When all the dignitaries, officers, and local volunteer Ukrainian militia, and volunteers from other villages were assembled in the marketplace, a short verdict was read pronouncing the death penalty (no causes, no crimes were announced) against the people who stood there tied hand and foot. A group of Einsatzkommando then simply mowed them down with submachine guns. The effect of this type of execution, whereby even German army officers were ordered to observe, was part of the Nazi psychological strategy; and was directed as much against their own citizens as against their enemies.

CHAPTER 14

THE CAMPS BELZEC AND JANOWSKA

(1941 - 1942) At the time I started working in Rawa Ruska, we were within a couple of miles from a place called Belzec. It wasn't very long before the people were talking about railroad cars full of people moving into a compound that was carefully guarded by the Nazi S.S., but coming out again empty. It was puzzling that there were hardly any prisoners or any kind of a "camp" or any facilities in Belzec. A big smokestack smoked day and night.

People were extremely fearful because the "Einzatz-Commandos" (Action Commandos) were roaming the countryside; and these self-sustaining units of killers were totally above any rules or regulations. They were professional killers recruited partially from criminal prisoners. They dressed in quasi police uniforms with submachine guns slung across their chests. I noted that Germans also feared them, because they were not subject to any military or Nazi Party command. They went where they wanted, and took whatever they wanted, even from German supply depots. Though they concentrated on killing Jews in the ghettos, they also did all kinds of other killings.

Though very little was actually known at the time, judging by the utmost secrecy and the fact that it was so well guarded by the elite German S.S., we were conscious that something very strange was going on at Belzec. No locals worked there. It was certain that the Germans were up to something nasty. But we could not in our wildest imaginations conceive the horrifying fact that they were shipping in people, gassing them, and then burning them in the crematorium. This was so mind-boggling that we could hardly come to this unspeakably inhuman conclusion, at first. The idea was incredible to imagine.

But before the winter of 1941-42 was over, we knew about the extermination camps, where cattle cars with barbed wire windows, full of people crying and calling for water, arrived and were shoved into factory buildings. We could observe only from a great distance because the whole surrounding area was off-limits to civilians. The factories had large smoke stacks, and rumor abounded that the cattle cars full of people were burned in there. We didn't know how this was done, but we did observe the cars full of people arriving there, and empty cars coming back.

Even in Lwow there were all kinds of rumors. Some people said that prisoners, and especially Jews, were taken to Rawa Ruska and electrocuted there. I knew these rumors were not true because I worked in Rawa Ruska. But Belzec was very near Rawa Ruska; it was a site where railways had access from Lwow, Krakow, and also the Warsaw region. The way to Belzec in the spring of 1942 became a place and time of horror. People could see horrendous scenes, especially the railway men. The Jews began to understand very well why they were being transported there, and on the journey they were given neither food nor water. At some of the stations you could see and hear the cries of the Jews offering 150 Zlotys, which was about a month's wages, for a kilo of bread. They would remove their gold finger rings and offer them in exchange for a glass of water for their children. The inhabitants of such cities as Lublin told of incredible scenes among the Jews. The S. S. shot the old, sick, lame, and halt on the spot, and transported thousands of others on to Belzec. It will never really be known how many people perished in transports or this extermination camp.

    My cousin Olek lived in Lwow and worked as a bookkeeper without his background ever being detected. Through him I was able to obtain some information about my father. He told me that my father had been caught during one of the frequent police manhunts, where people were rounded up, put them in a truck, and shipped away. No one really knew where. At one time they were shipped to Germany for slave labor, at other times to concentration camps.

While I worked in Rawa Ruska, first for the Polish firm Stronski, then for the German firm Stickel, I received one post-card from my mother, and one post-card and two letters from my father in the Janowska concentration camp with cries for help. He reported about himself in the 3rd person. The letters of my father were written in Polish and written in such guarded language that it was almost coded. I understood what he was trying to say, but it was not spelled out in a clear enough fashion for anyone else to understand. These were written so no one could detect they originated from a concentration camp. They were obviously smuggled out and dropped into a post box. It also must have meant a great amount of sacrifice on his part to come up with the value of a postage stamp, and then smuggle a letter out of camp. However, most concentration camps had organized so-called "Prisoner's Security Services."

My father described the fantastically cruel conditions there and said that he could not last long because of the lack of food and medical care. He also described the place of his work detail fairly accurately. He gave a distance of a half a kilometer up the road from a small railway station house near switch #31.

I still have this letter in a plastic envelope among my documents. It is extremely difficult to read it. I look at it every time I go through my papers, but I cannot bring myself to read it through from beginning to end. It is too painful; and I have avoided doing so for years.

He mentions that some of his clothing was stolen in the "showers" and that he is sick with either pneumonia or pleurisy. He continues that the only way to obtain medicine in the Janowska Concentration Camp is to buy it on the black market. To report to the clinic or the hospital would be tantamount to committing suicide. A friend who is a medical doctor recommended that he should buy the medicine, and the only way he could afford to do so was to let the doctor friend break the golden bridge out of his mouth to trade it for this medicine. He wonders whether he should do so. In any case, he says, I won't be able to last but a couple of months at maximum. As it turned out, he did not even last that long.

Travel was strictly regulated and many police patrols checked papers. I had no valid travel permits or reasons to go to Lwow, so I decided to borrow the small motorized bike that Firma Stickel used for messengers at their building sites. I used this little motor bike on several other occasions. It was extremely economical on fuel consumption, so after filling it up with about 5 quarts of gas/oil mix; I went in search of my father.

I had a loaf of black bread and some cooked meat in a rucksack on my back. I drove down the road to Lwow very carefully because I did not want to get stopped by either German or Ukrainian police patrols. That would have been extremely dangerous. In order to find the work detail, I had to drive past the main entrance of the Janowska concentration camp, and that in itself was an unsettling experience, since quite a few guards were standing and loitering around. From there I followed the railway track out and away from Lwow, until I recognized the small station master's house described in my father's letter. I found a ditch overgrown with bushes and brambles, and hid the motorbike there, and started walking.

Somehow, I had to be able to contact the prisoners without arousing the suspicion or alarm of the guards. As I came past switch #30, I noticed that further down at switch #31 there was some movement of people, and there was also an open 3-sided shack. I circled in order to approach this shack from the back side. I noticed a soldier, obviously an old man, standing in a uniform with a rifle with a fixed bayonet. In the wooden shack on a board sat three prisoners. At the track that ran in front of the shed, there were another four prisoners leaning on their shovels and picks. I worked my way slowly toward this group, advancing in the ditch so as not to be noticed. I could not distinguish who my father was among the prisoners. After waiting for some time, the old soldier walked down the track a little ways, and spoke to the prisoners who were standing around. I used this opportunity to approach the shack, and one of the prisoners rose, and although I could not believe my eyes, it was my father.

He was totally emaciated, a skeleton, obviously unable to do any meaningful work. Although he had not worn glasses, he now had a pair of glasses hanging on one ear piece. He shuffled toward me and we embraced and we whispered to one another. The other prisoners remained seated and did not move. They were in no better condition than my father. He had a prisoner's striped cap on his head, and also striped pants. Over it he wore his old winter coat. However, there was a 6 inch wide red stripe painted from collar to hem. He told me that the conditions were such that he did not think he could last more than two months.

I assured him that I would be back with some more food, and he should try to stay with this work detail, which seemed to be easier to approach than trying to break into the camp itself. I also told him that he should not give up hope, because I would try to rescue him if I found a way. We could spend only about five minutes together, because the guard came walking slowly back, and my father shuffled back to the bench, clutching the food I had brought him under his coat. I left the same way as I had approached and got back to my motorbike. I drove very slowly all the way back Rawa Ruska. It took me a long time. I was desperate! I could not imagine how I could rescue my poor father.

    What devastated me more than anything else was that, though I tried to figure out how to spirit my Father away (if only I could get hold of some means of transportation), no matter how I figured, there was no way that I could help him to escape, hide him, or deliver him to the Polish partisans. The Polish partisans were known not to accept any Jewish people, and particularly not those who needed recuperation, medication, and probably hospitalization. I knew no one anywhere with whom I could talk. The atmosphere was such that everyone was afraid, and this condition permeated every one of the communities, regardless of whether they were Jewish, Ukrainian, Polish or even German. Everyone was intimidated!

    The following week-end I could not go back to Janowska because I was on a work detail. The following Saturday, however, I had the time, but no access to the motorbike. I asked my boss, the Bauleiter Makarov, for a travel permit to Lwow, since I wanted to visit some friends. Although this was considered an insufficient reason to get a travel permit, he was kind enough to issue one to me. That in turn enabled me to go from Rawa Ruska to Lwow by train.

From the Lwow train station I had to walk several miles to find the little shed. Sure enough, here was again a work detail. This time, however, the guard was a Ukrainian S.S. man with a submachine gun across his chest. The approach was much more difficult. I alerted the prisoners in the shed by throwing a few small pebbles, and they somehow arranged that part of the detail walked down the railway track a very short distance, perhaps about 25 feet. That, in turn, made the guard walk along with them, and enabled me to have another meeting with my father, and transfer some bread and foodstuffs to him. We had very little time, and he warned me to be on the alert for the S.S. guard.

I tried to visit the concentration camp detail a third time after a couple of weeks, but there was no sign of anyone at the railway. I went to my cousin Olek in Lwow. He told me that he had heard that an epidemic of typhus had "occurred" and that the concentration camp at Janowska was totally liquidated, eradicated, and all prisoners were shot. I never saw my father again. Shortly thereafter, I shipped out to another building site of the German building firm Stickel in Luck in the Ukraine. I did not know it at the time, but a short time later they re-opened the concentration camp of Janowska and started their cruel game again.

After the War a prisoner of the Janowska concentration camp, Borwicz, who was rescued by the Polish underground, described this camp in his book. "Janowska Camp in Lwow was a "university" of torture. It can not be compared with Maidanek, Auschwitz, Dachau or Buchenwald, which could be described as "middle schools." "This camp was the heart of Hitlerian training in cruelty." The prisoners lived in barracks that were unheated and were terribly cold in winter. The whole camp had only one kitchen where a "soup" was given to the prisoners in the evening, and in the morning ersatz coffee and a piece of bread. The soup was often so stinky that, although they were very hungry, some of the prisoners would not eat it. Many of them became sick from it, and some died. The prison guards were mostly Ukrainians, some of them members of the **General Vlasof Division**. This was a Ukrainian Soviet General that went over to the German side. At the end of the war the "Vlasof" soldiers were forced to go back to Russia on Soviet ships. They were all summarily executed.

However, all command was in the hands of the S.S. officers. The hunger was indescribable. When the black bread was divided into small pieces of approximately 175 grams per prisoner, the little morsels that crumbled off were grabbed. Many fights broke out over the smallest crumbs. A combination of very hard work, lack of food, and psychological terrorism, such as waking the prisoners in the middle of the night to run to their work places, contributed to a large turn over -- meaning that many prisoners died or committed suicide. They were gathered up by a so-called "Todes-Brigade" (a death unit) and were taken to be burned. In the process of so many executions many of the people were not killed outright, but only wounded. They were gathered up along with the dead and thrown alive into the fires.

The ghetto community of Lwow sent packages to the prisoners because they were aware of the horrible conditions. Very little of the packages wound up in the hands of the prisoners. After the S.S. men helped themselves to whatever they wanted, the prison guards took the rest. During the time of my father's imprisonment at the Janowska Camp, the commandant of the camp was a young man of approximately 30 years from Berlin by the name of Fritz Gebauer. Like most commanding officers in this camp, he seems to have had some serious mental problems. Many of the S.S. men were obviously alcoholics. The rest, among them Gebauer, were plainly pathological mental cases. Gebauer was known by the prisoners as "the strangler." He was a mild looking and quietly speaking person. Occasionally he approached a prisoner and started to caress him around the neck after he took off his gloves. He became excited and strangled the prisoners with his bare hands. He had uncontrollable spasms while he was executing a prisoner this way. After a while, he straightened out his uniform, put on his gloves, and again appeared to be a very normal and kind, well behaved officer. During his trial it was testified that he ordered five prisoners to take off their clothes and climb into a large barrel of water. The temperature was -27 C (-10 F). He timed them as they froze to death.

 I have always questioned how it was possible that the Third Reich was able to mobilize virtually thousands of maniacal torturers and mass murderers. None of the existing documentation left after the Nueremberg War Crimes Trials, or even the Eichmann trial in Jerusalem, nor the Yad Vashem, has ever answered this question.

 The Janowska Camp at its peak had approximately 8,000 prisoners. There were constantly further shipments from small villages and towns all over Galicja, and through a sorting system the camp was able to keep the number of prisoners steady. The weaker, or those in any way sick were transported to a field on a little hill not far away from the camp and were shot and buried. From the beginning of the camp there were also constant transports to the nearby town of Belzec, which was a gas liquidation camp. During the entire time of the existence of Camp Janowska from the end of 1941 until July 1944, the amount of sadistic murders within the camp has never been established, but it was known to be in the tens of thousands. On a daily basis prisoners were beaten to death or shot with pistols and rifles. One of the commandants made sport of shooting prisoners with his rifle from the balcony of his villa, in the presence of his wife and 4-year-old daughter. She clapped her hands and jumped up and down when he killed a prisoner outright. After the war Gebauer was caught and put before a war tribunal in Poland as a war criminal and was executed by hanging.

  The commandants of this camp, S.S. Untersturmfuhrer Willhaus, and Unterscharfuhrer Rokita were transferred in 1942 or 43 to the eastern front, and according to records lost their lives during the fighting there. Willhaus, during a nervous attack while inspecting a jail in Lacki, jumped out of a window of the prison. He was only slightly injured. These mental cases had undisputed power of life and death (mostly the latter) over thousands of prisoners.

The post-card that I received from my Mother was written in German, and for that reason, I felt compelled to destroy it. I did so regretfully, for it was too dangerous for me to be in possession of a post-card written in German, as I was pretending to be a Polish youngster, born and raised in a small Polish village with poor knowledge of the German language.

My Mother joyfully telling me that she had found employment as a seamstress in Rawa Ruska and that she would be shipped there to start her "job." It did not take me very long to put things together. I realized that she would come from Lwow to Belzec, passing Rawa Ruska. The people, whoever they were, told her that "job" story so she would not realize that she would wind up in that unspeakable place. It struck me unbearably that this amounted to the virtual execution of my dear Mother. The post-card from my Mother was the last I ever heard of her. Inquiries after the war produced absolutely nothing. She was shipped to Belzec. She disappeared!

Belzec was so secret that to this day the number annihilated is unknown. Only <u>ONE</u> prisoner survived!!

The naive description from my Mother that she was being deported to an imaginary "job," the capture by the Gestapo of my roommate, Janek, and his disappearance without a trace -- made me realize that I was quite on my own. I could not look to anyone for help or support, and I could not even ask anyone for any advice.

After the War through searching for my mother and other relatives, and my involvement in rescuing concentration camp inmates, I became thoroughly acquainted with the concentration camp networks from one end of Europe to the other. It was odd that shortly after the War I did not come across the name of Janowska. The reason may have been that it was of relatively short duration, and the eradication of this camp was so complete that there were very few survivors, if any. The guards of the camp were Ukrainians, Lithuanians and Latvians. In the case of Janowska, they did most of the dirty work for the Germans. But the command was exclusively in the hands of the German S.S. The great misfortune was that my father found himself in this hell and perished without a trace.

CHAPTER 15

THE BUTCHERS OF RAWA RUSKA

At the beginning of December I decided that I had better find a new job. Stronski, my first employer in Rawa Ruska, was cutting its labor force because there wasn't enough work for Polish construction firms to go around in the winter. Such a layoff would be dangerous for me.

Rather than wait for the Arbeitsamt, the German labor administration to look at my papers again and assign me a job that I would have to accept, I began looking around myself. I talked to some other workers in town and soon learned that a German building firm -- owned by one Dr. Engineer Wilhelm Stickel of Berlin -- treated people more decently than other companies. The Stickel firm still operated through the winter and supplied its personnel with some food. This had great appeal to me, for in the late fall workers at Stronski had already been starving. Forced by hunger to steal potatoes from the peasants fields, we roasted them in tiny fires right out in the fields to supplement our meager diet.

Because of my officially "limited but workable" knowledge of German I had a relatively easy time landing a job at Stickel in their stockroom. German was actually my mother tongue, having been born and raised in Vienna, Austria, and going to school there. But as "Taduesz Chwistek, a Pole of moderate circumstances, I could not afford to know German too well. I worked hard to speak broken German with a strong accent, to use bad grammar and a very limited vocabulary. I carried German textbooks around and was seen studying a lot. I "picked up" new expressions from my German co-workers and used them comically, and asked for tickets to watch German movies. Gradually, my German "improved," and because I could speak Polish and some Ukrainian as well, people in Stickel began to use me for various errands.

Ironically, they continued to converse privately in German in my presence, oftentimes unconsciously revealing important information -- in their peculiar mind-set assuming that, like all members of "inferior races" such as Poles, Ukrainians, Russians, I would not understand what they were saying.

The building used by Stickel was located in a modern house on one of the main streets on the outskirts of Rawa Ruska. It was a converted store with apartments above. In the first floor office several local girls, Polish and Ukrainian, worked preparing the payroll, making requisitions, and putting together all the paperwork necessary in dealing with the German authorities. They also handled the very important food stamp situation.

The warehouse in the basement was my realm. I presided over machine parts, nails, bolts, screws, wires, electrical connectors, timers, detonators and a multitude of other hardware that the firm used. Only explosives were out of my reach, but later on I had access to dynamite and other explosives..

Upstairs were the offices of Mr. Makarov, the "Bauleiter" or building chief, a handsome White Russian who was in charge of this branch of the Stickel firm. His parents had escaped in 1918 during the Bolshevik Revolution from Russia to Prague, Czechoslovakia. His secretary, about 30, was a tall, thin, pale, sickly and always unhappy Miss Irmgard from the German province of Thuringia. Though she wasn't very attractive, she had a "fiancée" somewhere in the German army, and defended herself quite successfully from the advances Mr. Makarov continuously made towards her, probably out of sheer boredom. Slowly, Mr. Makarov began using me to run certain personal errands for him. These errands enabled me to get into town, and even sometimes to other cities, such as Lwow, to procure things on the black market that he could send back to his wife and daughter in Braunschweig, Germany.

Of all the local employees, only one Polish girl and I spoke reasonably good German, so we found ourselves invited upstairs quite often for ersatz coffee and after-work chats. At one of these gatherings we discussed the appearance of a strange military unit in town.

We were all very conscious of uniforms. Not only the local indigent population and people in hiding, like I was, but also German civilians were apprehensive, looking out for various regiments. We instantly recognized the German military and police. The basic color of the Wehrmacht, the army, was medium green (the so-called "feldgrau") while the Luftwaffe, the air force, sported bluish gray. We could distinguish at a glance between the Waffen S.S., fighting unit of the S.S. in camouflage battle dress, and the regular S.S., clad in black. We knew the difference between the S.D., a secret police that collaborated with the S.S. and the actual secret police, the Gestapo.

But the unsavory-looking characters that came in army trucks into Rawa Ruska in February of '42 were wearing uniforms that weren't either army or police. The epaulettes and collars on their green jackets were the army type; their large pistol holders were the police type. Strange insignia on their caps said "Einsatzgruppen" -- special action group. But what action? The army was fighting in Smolensk at that time -- that to me was "action!"

As they got out of their brand-new freshly painted Mercedes trucks with rifles and suitcases by their sides, they looked like a bunch of German butchers -- rather heavy set, pink-faced and apparently half drunk. Soon they were swaggering all around the place. Other Germans stayed out of their way and showed very visible disdain for those people. I soon understood from conversations overheard among the Germans that members of the Einsatzgruppen were believed to be criminals, pardoned in exchange for joining that organization. Still, no one knew what they were there for.

Then, after the Einsatzgruppen were established in Rawa Ruska, the commander of the Wehrmacht garrison in town issued an order that was posted on the walls in all public places: a curfew for ALL inhabitants would be enforced around the clock over the next three days. The text in three languages -- German, Ukrainian, and Polish -- made it clear that NO ONE was exempt, not even Germans. This was unusual and frightening.

The next morning at 7:00 A.M. we met as usual in the Stickel offices. Since our living quarters were located across a back courtyard, we could sneak into the building without showing ourselves on the street. Going out on the street was forbidden under penalty of death. We didn't know what else to do, or what to expect, so we just sat there and waited. Outside it was quiet.

Suddenly, from the direction of the Ghetto, we heard rifle shots, which ended abruptly. Then a few more. Then the burp of a machine gun. Voices -- crying, wailing, yelling. We could not make out the words. The Ghetto was about a half mile away from the Stickel building, but we were close enough to hear the cacophony of horror and despair, shrieks of panicked women, the thin voices of crying children, the chilling screams of men.

As we sat there horrified, we no longer had any illusions about what was taking place in the Ghetto. Over the next several hours as we sat there paralyzed in deadly silence, the shooting continued sporadically. Around noon, Miss Irmgard asked us to come to her office for coffee. All of us -- the three German and two Polish foremen, three office girls and I -- went upstairs and found the secretary frightened out of her wits and in a state of severe shock. She was paler than ever, and had obviously thrown up in the bathroom moments before. She avoided looking in the direction of the window.

I decided to take a cautious glance at the street. I saw a cart, the kind commonly used by peasants to carry potatoes or coal, drawn by a skinny, half-starved horse with a wooden yoke around its neck. The horse was led by a Jewish "Ghetto policeman" who walked holding the animal by the bit. The open wagon was filled with human bodies -- men and women covered with gashes and bullet wounds, their tongues hanging out, children with crushed skulls -- all just tossed on top of one another. The bodies were still, limp, twisted into the most grotesque positions, with their arms and legs sticking akimbo out of the cart, which left a trail of blood on the pavement.

    The operations of the Einsatzgruppen continued in shifts day and night, and the carts passed in an endless procession, dripping blood until the street was covered with it. The blood darkened fast, and we could smell it in our room. Even though Miss Irmgard had prepared a lot of food, none of us touched it.

    We didn't talk much. We couldn't sleep. If we dozed off for a few minutes at night it was only to be jerked awake by another barrage of shots. We hovered between fear, revulsion, and boredom, having no work to do during those days. All we could do was sit and wait.

    Despite all the brainwashing and political indoctrination they had received, the Germans in our group seemed fearful and ashamed. They were unprepared to endorse the kind of atrocity going on before their very eyes. One of the elderly foremen, normally of a quiet disposition, told me that he had witnessed the Bialystock Gestapo hanging Jewish laborers by a rope drawn under their armpits -- a painful punishment -- to make those exhausted slaves work harder. That had been ugly enough, but still short of mass murder. "This thing now," he mumbled, "is not worthy of Germany." Then, regretting this moment of frankness, he withdrew again into his shell. The other two Germans sat there in gloom, while Makarov, quite the coward, hid in his office and never stuck his head out.

Miss Irmgard was in bad shape, near hysteria. She vomited again and could not sleep. She wondered aloud "how such a thing could ever be explained or justified." She told us that revenge for this crime could very well become a big problem after the War. Immediately after this period of mass murder she applied for a transfer from Rawa Ruska, convinced that assignment to Germany, France, or anywhere in Western Europe would be preferable. Perhaps she was correct. Eastern Poland and Russia were the foremost killing fields of World War II. The rest of the continent didn't witness comparable atrocities.

As for me, I had to employ all my psychological resources not to betray myself during those endless hours of horror. I had to exercise utmost control to maintain my usual bland composure. I never spoke my mind and avoided any kind of political discussion, explaining when pressed that I could not understand some of the more complicated words in German. Since they could not communicate with me, some of the Germans lost interest in questioning me. It was important to show some compassion, but not too much. I had no doubt at all that some of those people, upset though they were about the butchery, would not hesitate to denounce me to the Gestapo if they were to suspect anything at all.

To get away from them and stop thinking I made the excuse to go downstairs to my storeroom to make an inventory. Instead, alone into the basement, I fell into a stupor. I couldn't cry, scream, or curse. I felt empty. Nothingness. Only later in life did I learn that when we face extreme circumstances with which we feel helpless to cope, so-called "normal" human reactions are often suspended. Some merciful defensive psychological mechanism numbs us. I can only hope that something of this kind also made it easier for the victims of the Rawa Ruska ghetto to meet their unbearable fate.

We had no electrical power, so we burned candles and sat by kerosene lamps at night. We could not see much of the Ghetto from our vantage point, but the bursts of shots, the never ending cries, and the flickering fires kept us aware of the situation. We could not see the destination of the wagons carrying the bodies, either, but we guessed, quite correctly, that they all headed toward dirt pits on the western outskirts of town. We were aware of those pits because the Germans were always busy shooting someone in Rawa Ruska, and disposing of them there. One day teachers would be targeted, the next Communists. Partisans, sabotage suspects, anyone for any random reason. They had so many enemies to kill. All the victims were buried in the same place.

Workers in the nearby barracks told us later that the horse drawn carts were led to the pits. The Jewish "Ghetto police" threw the bodies in while army trucks dumped lime on the remains. One layer was covered with dirt and another layer thrown in. Empty carts returned to the Ghetto for the next load, and the procedure continued until the third day there was only silence on the other side of the bloodied road. The Jewish "Ghetto Police" in their civilian clothes and blue police caps were lined up on the sides of the ditches and machine gunned down. When the firing ended, the last chore of the Einsatzgruppen of Rawa Ruska was completed.

When the curfew was lifted and we went about our business in town, the Ghetto was looted by the local Ukrainian population. There had been a tremendous amount of physical destruction, but otherwise the ghetto was abandoned and eerily silent, a windswept site of mass murder. The traveling murder squad was already gone. The members packed up their suitcases, tossed them into their Mercedes trucks, and moved on to their next task in some provincial town of Eastern Galicja or the Ukraine, to liquidate another Ghetto.

    Although the Germans in their inimitable fashion were keeping meticulous count of their various operations and the Einsatzgruppen reported their kill weekly, neatly divided into categories -- so many thousand men, so many women, so many children -- the totals involved remain unknown. I am convinced that the Einsatzgruppen murder squads were directly responsible for the killing of hundreds of thousands of Jews, as well as quite a few other peoples. They had license to kill anyone they wanted to.

    Though I witnessed unbelievable cruelty, disgusting atrocities, shockingly inhuman behavior, the butchery of these Einsatzgruppen was probably one of the worst things I have ever seen in my life. After the war German apologists tried to tell me that the German Army had nothing to do with the extermination of Jews and other people, and were not involved in war crimes. The German Army supervised some of these preparatory actions and actively supported the S.S. and the Einsatzgruppen in their nefarious activities.

I learned after the War of "Operation Barbarossa" through reading the history of the German attack upon the Soviet Union in 1941, that the S.S. prepared special killing squads known as Einsatzgruppen, and also sought and organized local collaborators among the Lithuanians, Latvians and Ukrainians to help in mass murders.

One of the many grim and revolting pictures in a book I picked in a London bookstore about he Holocaust in Europe, gave me a particular shock. It was of an Einsatzgruppen murder squad who had arrived at their place of work in an eastern Galicjan town in the autumn of 1941. There they stood in their police uniforms, 9 mm submachine guns strapped across their chests, pistols in their belts, and suitcases at their sides. They were issued special rations of vodka -- I suppose as an anesthetic to aid them in performing their criminal butchery.

Events in Rawa Ruska convinced me that there was absolutely no hope that the Germans would let any Jews live, although there were constantly cruel promises to that effect to the Ghetto population -- they were told they were necessary to the War effort. Later, through most unusual circumstances, I got hold of a Walter PPK semi-automatic pistol, which I carried on me for the duration of the War. I would have used it unhesitatingly against anyone who threatened my life or to expose my identity.

    During my various travels throughout eastern Poland and western Russia I observed many strange S. S. "military"(?) units. Somehow they were always at or near concentration camps or prisoner of war camps. They had shoulder patches showing that they belonged to an Arab Legion, a Lithuanian Legion, a Latvian Legion, and even a unit from Flanders (Belgium). They were all VOLUNTEERS!

    It is a mystery to me until today how Nazi Germany was able to assemble such a number of thousands of war criminals. All types of explanations answer this question only partly. They recruited among the criminals, letting them out of prison, gave them weapons and authority to kill, maim, rob, rape, torture and pillage in the occupied territories. An unsavory preparation that lasted for several years conditioned the young people in Germany through Nazi propaganda to hatred, contempt of human life, especially of strangers, such as Jews, Gypsies, Slavs, extending this theory to Communists, homosexuals, and what they termed "undesirables." That included disabled or mentally ill Germans as well. Actually, the system functioned only too well.

This is one of the main reasons why the Holocaust was treated mostly with silence between 1945 and the late 1960's.

On the other hand, I have difficulty understanding that in some situations hundreds or even thousands of prisoners could be held in terror by a handful of S.S. guards. If all of them had run in all directions, they would surely have overpowered a few armed soldiers and perhaps saved many by fleeing into the forests. This is obviously easier said than done. The lack of organization, the poor physical condition, and above all, the psychological conditioning convincing the prisoners that they were helpless, abandoned and powerless did them in.

CHAPTER 16

MARIAN

In the fall of 1939 - 40 during the Soviet occupation of Lwow both in my downtown school as well as in the Sapieha High School, one of my friends was Marian.

Marian was a very strong boy, about a head taller than the rest of us in the class, and built like an ox. He was the most gentle and peaceful fellow I have ever met. We became good friends, and since like most boys we were often involved in all kinds of disputes and fights, Marian's was an absolute peacemaker. The bullies were afraid to attack friends of Marian because of his size and strength; and his quiet disposition contributed towards settling any kind of misunderstanding or disagreement.

After school we often played volley ball and soccer, and in the soccer matches, Marian was chosen as goalkeeper. Though he was slow, his size covered more space than anyone else could cover within the space of the goal.

After I went to Rawa Ruska under my assumed name of Chwistek, I stood in line at a grocery store to obtain my ration of bread and sausage, and whatever else they had to offer on that day. Someone touched me from behind on my shoulder, and to my greatest astonishment, there stood Marian. He made some kind of a face at me, obviously not wanting to be openly recognized or greeted, or to engage in any conversation in that spot for reasons of safety. I understood immediately that Marian, a Jew, was also like myself traveling on false documents.

    I kept standing quietly in line and after I made my purchases I walked away very slowly, waiting for him to catch up with me. He quietly told me he was staying outside of town in a barracks belonging to one of the building firms. On Sunday evenings there usually was no one in the barracks. All the workers went to town to get drunk or enjoy themselves in any way they could. If I wanted to stop and say "hello" to him, he would be there waiting for me. I agreed, and we went our various ways. It was very dangerous for us to meet, because both of us were vulnerable to exposure. If one of us were caught, it would have back-lashed on the other, and the repercussions were always deadly. It was known that interrogation of hidden Jews was always done with extreme torture by both the Germans and the Ukrainians.

    Nevertheless, the following Sunday I set out on foot and walked three miles out on the westerly road from Rawa Ruska. This took me to the barracks, which were right next to the "killing grounds" where the carts full of dead bodies were taken. There the "Ghetto Police" who transported the carts were also summarily executed by the "Butchers of Rawa Ruska," the Einsatzgruppen.

Sure enough, Marian was waiting on one of the primitive bunk beds, with sisal bags filled with straw as mattresses. These were the quarters for the building workers of his outfit. We embraced one another, we were so happy to meet again. I asked, "How did it go with you?" He replied, "As soon as they moved my parents and me into the Ghetto, they caught me in one of their round-ups; but I managed to escape before they could ship me out." I told him, "You know, the same thing happened to me, twice -- once on "Petlura Day," and again about three weeks later.

"Petlura Day" took place on July, 1941 shortly after the invasion of the Germans into Lwow. Thousands of men and women were seized, ostensibly for forced labor, but most of them were taken to prisons in the city and beaten to death by local Ukrainians in a three-day orgy. It was said that they wanted to "avenge" the murder of Simon Petlura fifteen years before. Petlura, an exiled Ukrainian leader was assassinated in Paris in 1926. Petlura organized gangs in 1919 after World War I, and his gangs killed at least 60,000 Jews in various Ukrainian towns.

Marian told me, "Mostly young people, students were being rounded up and arrested by the Ukrainian police, supposedly to be shipped to work camps."

I told Marian, "During the Petlura Action I was also caught. The special arm band showing me to be an employed worker didn't help at all either. Two policemen were going door to door searching the large apartment buildings for young people. One was supposedly watching the crowd of about 20 of us who were standing in the street waiting to be shipped to whatever destination awaited us. I waited and watched my chance, and whenever he turned away for a moment, I inched closer to a walled garden. Finally, he was called by the other policemen to come help search, and I threw myself over the 5 foot wall, and fell into the bushes on the other side. I didn't think any of the other men waiting had noticed me, because they were focused on the policemen going into the apartment on the other side of the street. I waited for a while and then slowly crawled through the garden into the next street. I hid there for an hour, and when things quieted down, I went back to my parents. They were overjoyed to see me, as they had been terribly worried." It later became known that the young people who had been rounded up on Petlura Day were taken to the police headquarters in Lwow, and several thousand were murdered there by the Ukrainian police on that day.

Marian said, "Yes, I know. They seem to change the rules as they go along. First they told me that if I had working papers I would be safe; but that turned out to be a lie. There just is no future in Lwow for any of us." I replied, "I think that the Belzec Extermination Camp will be our end if we get caught." Marian answered, "You know, shortly after we moved to Lwow they caught my parents, and they disappeared -- without a trace. I also have a sister, but I don't know where she is. I'm working here for this building firm, but the conditions are very harsh, very tough. The work is so hard and the food is so little. I don't know what I am going to do. I don't think that we'll see one another any more, because I am going to try to move away from Rawa Ruska. It is too close to Lwow. I was born and raised in these parts, and there are too many people who know me. But I would like to meet with you after the War. I hope we can both survive this terrible time, and there will be an end to it someday. For us to find one another after the War, we should put a little ad in the "Lwowska Gazeta (which was a little newspaper in Lwow), and this way we will find one another. I said, "That's a good idea. Let's try and do it!"

He told me, "One of the things that bothers me the most in this barracks is that we have so many fleas." I said, "I don't know why that is. I don't have any, and we haven't had this problem in our barracks." I lifted up the straw mattress, and the boards underneath it were almost black with fleas. "I have never seen anything like it in my life," I told him. "I don't know what to do about it really, but there must be some kind of ammonia or something that you can try to get hold of to eliminate them."

He told me, "Other than this flea problem, I feel pretty healthy -- in pretty good shape. But if I stay here too long, I won't, because the food is just not sufficient to keep me going with the work pace that they demand here." I replied, "I'm much luckier than that, though my food situation is not much better than yours. Since I transferred from the Polish to the German building firm, my work situation has improved considerably. At the German firm I no longer have to go out into the fields working, but I am working in the store rooms and around the offices, so there is nowhere near the great physical effort necessary."

We also exchanged news about some other friends -- our good friend "Tolek" (who later after the War became president of the International division of a large American pharmaceutical firm located in Switzerland). He had somehow left

Lwow with his parents toward the west. We didn't know what had happened to him at the time. Our other friend "Nolek" had an uncle in the Soviet Union in Moscow, and this uncle had managed to whisk his parents and him out somewhere to the east into Russia.

We had a good visit, embraced and wished one another luck, and have never heard of one another again.

In 1945 after the War, there was no "Gazeta Lwowska," and Lwow became part of the Soviet Union -- as a matter of fact a city where foreigners up until the late 1970's were not allowed to visit.

1. VIENNA (AUSTRIA)
2. WARSAW (POLAND)
3. KRAKOW (POLAND)
4. LWOW-LEMBERG-LVIV
   (POLAND-UKRAINE)
5. RAWA RUSKA
   (POLAND-UKRAINE)
   (BELZEC EXTERMINATION CAMP)

6. LUCK (POLAND-UKRAINE)
7. SIMFEROPOL (UKRAINE)
   (CAPITAL OF CRIMEA)
8. KERCH (CAUCASUS)
9. BERLIN (GERMANY)
10. UDINE (ITALY)
    (BUIA, OSOPPO, GEMONA)
11. BAD ISCHL (AUSTRIA)

CHAPTER 17

LUCK – HORROR YEAR 1942

Rawa Ruska had become a hellhole for me. Going to visit my cousin Olek in Lwow, I was in a constant state of anxiety and fear that my identity would be discovered. The weather had turned very bad, and the mud on the mostly unpaved streets and the dirt that prevailed all over, made life extremely uncomfortable. There was nothing but grayness all around. We worked in the morning, without interest and unenthusiastically, for there really was not much to do. The only break in the monotony were my conversations with the German secretary and also the Polish secretary in the offices of Stickel. The Polish secretary, Maria, had a German soldier boyfriend, and had great guilt feelings, about which she told me. The soldier had left for the Russian front and she had not heard from him. I thought her attachment to him was overly optimistic -- because he would probably not come back to her one way or another.

My boss, Engineer Makarov, was recalled to Berlin to prepare for another assignment to a new building site. Firma Stickel constantly obtained new road building contracts from the Organization Todt, which were very profitable for them. They were always behind the front fixing up roads and bridges and airstrips, and moved their personnel around as needed.

I hoped to get transferred from Rawa Ruska to almost ANYWHERE -- to get out of this terrible location. I was constantly afraid of meeting people who knew me and would denounce me. I carried a Walther 7.65 semi-automatic pistol, which in itself was a dangerous thing for a Pole to have. I kept it fully loaded with the trigger cocked, with just the safety latch on, so that I could use it if anyone threatened me.

I also feared that the Gestapo might come back, if by chance they had not executed Janek and had sent him instead to a concentration camp. If they questioned him further, he would certainly not be able to hold back information that would kill me.

Our supervisor at that time, Mr. Wehrmann, a man in his 50's, was an old-line road building technician. He spoke quite freely about his previous experiences at various locations for the firm. One of them was Bialowiez, which was a hunting preserve of the Presidents of Poland; which after the victorious occupation of Poland by the Germans had become the property of Hermann Goering. Stickel was engaged there in building some roads, and he told us that Makarov supervised the work there. They had used mostly

Jewish slave labor to work on these projects. Because of the poor rations the half starved people did this heavy work too slowly, which upset the timing scheduling of the work Makarov was supposed to have done. Consequently, Wehrmann reported, Makarov resorted to rather severe punishments to make them worker harder, faster. Some he had whipped. Others he hung in trees by their armpits. This was supposed to set an example to the starved workers to exert themselves more, in order to fulfill the orders he had received.

    I never after that heard anything more on the subject and do not know to what extent Mr. Makarov was personally responsible and to what extent the punishments were meted out. In the overview of the atrocities committed by the General Government (German occupied part of Poland) the above misdeeds were relatively minor. Comparing actions was complex at best, and not being there personally, it was difficult to pass judgment. But it was an item that bothered me very much at the time, and especially after the war when Makarov asked me to testify on his behalf that he had not engaged in any kind of Nazi activities or atrocities.

    I asked Mr. Makarov to be kind enough to try and get me transferred when he got to Berlin, because I wanted to advance my career -- or so I told him. I received communications from the office that I was eligible to move to their building site in Luck, now in the Ukraine, but before the outbreak of the War had belonged to Poland. It was the border area between Poland and the Soviet Ukraine. I was happy to accept the transfer, since it would take me out of Rawa Ruska to an area where it was highly unlikely that anyone knew me.

{Even before the German killing squads reached some of the regions in the Ukraine and Lithuania, the local population often attacked the Jews. These attacks were not pogroms to beat and loot, but to kill -- to destroy a whole community in one swift blow. The records of these attacks are scant because few Jews survived to recount what happened. In some of the smaller villages as soon as the Red Army withdrew and before the Germans arrived, the Ukrainians fell upon the Jewish families. The ferocity of the hatred of the Ukrainians was not only directed against Jews. Russian prisoners of war were also murdered in cold blood.

In 1996 a documentary film and display traveled from museum to museum in Germany depicting the participation of the regular German Army in the atrocities of the eastern occupied territories. It met with ferocious protests, not only by Neo-Nazis, but all kinds of right-wing and patriotic Germans. The legend persists that the

Army held no taint of the atrocities committed by the S.S., S.D., Gestapo, and Einsatzkommandos.}

In December prior to my arrival at Luck, the Jews were herded into a labor camp. They found out that they were to be "liquidated" the following day, and a very uneven battle ensued. Some of the defenders were killed, and the rest were shot afterwards. By the time I got into Luck, the town was "Judenrein" -- cleared of all Jews.

It was a very eerie experience to visit parts of the various towns and villages where the Kommandos had gone through and done their mass killings. The houses that were not burned to the ground were just empty. There was no furniture in them, or any kind of personal possession. It was obvious that in every instance, whether it were in Rawa Ruska or in Luck or in any of the other villages I had seen in the Ukraine, that the local population went in immediately after the mass murders and looted and picked everything clean. There wasn't a curtain rod, a piece of furniture, or any kind of kitchen utensil left. Even toilets, toilet seats and water faucets were torn out. It was particularly shocking to see that in these empty rooms the only things that were noticeable were bullet holes and large dark splotches of blood.

A few days later I packed my few belongings and bid my acquaintances in Rawa

Ruska good-by. I went to the railway station and took a local from Rawa Ruska to Lwow, and another dirty and slow train from Lwow back out to Luck. During the stop-over in Lwow I went to see my cousin Olek. He was a splendid person, and I always remember him in his younger days in his dapper military uniform. We have been close and loving friends throughout our lifetimes.

    On arrival in Luck, I asked directions and walked out to the Firma Stickel, where I reported to their offices in a compound with a low surrounding wall. I was assigned a berth in one of the nearby houses with the rest of the Polish workers. Our newly nailed together bunks each had a sack of straw as a mattress.

    I then reported to Mr. Peters, who was 6'4" tall and very thin. He came from the port city of Bremen and had one of those "Schmidt" caps on at all times. He was a very severe man, but he tried always to be correct. He lived in the compound with his wife, and was the boss of the various work gangs. He questioned me at length and I replied in fairly good German. I was able to "improve" my German rather quickly there, because no one knew how well or badly I spoke German before -- so I could take a giant leap forward to make things a little easier. I still spoke with a foreign accent and pretended to be tongue tied at times, and searched for words.

There was always a shortage of interpreters in the many locations where I worked, not only for the building firm Stickel but in general. The laborers and workmen were of mixed nationalities, unable to understand the German managers or officials. Consequently, especially in those remote areas of eastern Russia or western Poland, called Volhynia, someone speaking any of the languages, such as Polish or Ukrainian, who also understood or spoke German, was in demand. That was also one of the reasons why my position was always quite a bit better than most of the other fellow Polish conscripted laborers.

One of the first tasks I was assigned was to drive a truck with the Polish workers to the building sites, drop them off and later to pick them up again and bring them back to the worker's quarters. Mr. Peters made that decision quickly because he said, "Well, we need you to drive these workers because you speak Polish and Ukrainian." No one bothered to ask me if I knew how to drive or if I had a license. They just assumed I could handle a large sized truck. In the morning the workers assembled and got onto the truck and I drove to the three building sites where they were repairing roads and railway tracks. I took the truck back empty, and around 6:00 P.M. I went in reverse and picked them all up again.

During one of these trips I was stopped by a police patrol consisting of two German policemen and one Ukrainian. The police patrols were mixed, as was the administration; this part of the Ukraine being administered by a German civilian administration parallel to a local Ukrainian one. I was asked for a driver's license, which I did not have. After long discussions, I was told that I was to return to my firm with the truck and see to it that I got a driver's license. I reported the incident to Mr. Peters, and after I had delivered my workers the next day, he let me use the truck to go into town to obtain a driver's license. I went to the town offices and reported to the police station to show my documents, which indicated that I was a Pole. Again great discussions, the result if which was that they were reluctant to give me any kind of permit or document. I asked to telephone my boss at Stickel where I reported to Mr. Peters that the police would not issue me a driver's license. Perhaps he wished to talk to the commanding sergeant of the post. I turned the telephone over, and heard some very loud yelling and screaming. After this "conversation" I was given a driving test (which consisted of going down the road and back). I was issued a German driving permit for both passenger cars and trucks. This was also an amazing document. Under the German administration, no "less than human" Poles or

Russians were allowed to drive, and were therefore not issued permits. I got out of those offices just as fast as I could, and scurried back to our firm, where I reported that now everything was in good order and I could legally drive the truck.

In 1945 after the collapse of the Third Reich, I found myself in Austria. I took this driver's license, issued in Luck, Ukraine, and obtained an Austrian driver's license in its place, with my picture on it. This new driver's license was then in my real name, Gleisner, and not Chwistek.

I must have impressed Mr. Peters because my papers showed that I was not just a common laborer, but that I managed the magazine (warehouse) of Stickel in Rawa Ruska. He pronounced that I would not have to live in the bunkhouse with the other workers, but assigned me a room in another house with the German truck drivers -- a much more comfortable place with a shower and toilet in the hallway. It was a stone house, and my room also had a bunk bed with a real mattress. During my entire stay in Luck, I lived alone in that room. I would say that under the circumstances the accommodations were decidedly luxurious!

My work started the following morning, and it was not very hard. They were also marking time to a great degree. However, there were a few developments in Luck. The Ukrainian Partisans became active and constantly blew up the trains entering and leaving Luck. The trains had to go very slowly and carry an extra car in front of the locomotive for a bomb to blow up instead of the locomotive. The Partisans, of course, figured that one out very quickly. They just installed longer timing devices on their bombs so that they blew up the locomotive anyway. Whole trains were derailed regularly.

There were also attacks on the police stations and municipal administration offices in the area. Therefore, we were issued ancient rifles to protect the Stickel compound at night, and we had to have a change of guards. To my great surprise they also issued a rifle to me. They asked me if I knew how to shoot it, and though I had little previous experience, I replied, "Yes." And it was left at that.

We were supposed to sit below the low wall surrounding the compound at night and observe the opposite side of a broad road that contained the cemetery, which the Partisans used successfully to approach the city. Our bosses thought that there might also be an attack on the Stickel compound. If I had to shoot, I was going to shoot high not to hit anyone, and who would know the difference? Nothing happened, however, much to my relief.

After having been in Luck for a few months, I received a note from my friend, Marie in the Rawa Ruska office. She wanted me to help her transfer to Luck because she was very bored in Rawa Ruska with hardly any work to do. Though their work came to an end, they kept the offices open there. I was unable to help her transfer.

In Luck I also heard horror stories about the "Einsatzgruppen" who had come there a few months earlier and performed a massacre that few were likely to forget. The ghastly murders of babies and children, rapes and mutilations were told with a deep fear and loathing of the Germans. Only a few people were glad that the Jews got killed. I was glad to have missed that episode, having endured through the one in Rawa Ruska. Was it better than Rawa Ruska? The difference was, there was some resistance.

CHAPTER 18

MAROONED ON THE CRIMEA

In the summer of 1943, suddenly, after only a few months in Luck (in the Ukraine), I was given orders to go to the headquarters of Firma Stickel in Berlin!

I was issued a "MARSCHBEFEHL" (Military Marching Order). With this document the rail road station issued rail tickets. At all bigger stops or layovers it also entitled the bearer to food and overnight quarters at a military barracks or a hotel.

This was the first time I saw Berlin. The train journey took over two days, with many changes. Upon arriving in Berlin I discovered that the firm had accepted a road building contract in the Crimea, functioning under the command of the quasi-military building units of the "ORGANISATION TODT," named after the founder, Ing. (Engineer) Todt. Since this was a far out location for the first time in the activities of Stickel, the staff was supplied uniforms from the O. T.

The Organization Todt was formed before the outbreak of the War as a para-military organization of work battalions to build roads, bridges, and airport runways to support and

Wehrmacht. They were not a military unit in the strict sense of the word because they had no arms of any significance, and they also were not organized in a military sense. The German military command did not want to have German civilians or Polish, Russian or Ukrainian forced labor working in the areas near the front in civilian clothing. The workers needed to be easily recognizable. Consequently the building firms contracted with the military command for building projects. Firma Stickel in Rawa Ruska, for instance, contracted with the German army to build roads in a large area that were used for tank proving rounds and military exercises. Since this area was far away from military action there was no need to get incorporated into the Organisation Todt.

      However, when Stickel got a contract to build or rebuild roads and bridges or construct runways in the Crimea, the firm was ordered to get their personnel and all their procedures incorporated into the O. T. framework. It was envisioned that Stickel would have to do some of this work on the other side of the Straits of Kerch in the Caucasus. Because Germany was desperately short of gasoline and diesel fuel, the aim of the German strategy and their ultimate goal was to capture the oil fields in the Caucasus. From the very beginning of the war I think these objectives were planned and pursued. But the Germans never reached this goal.

Germany was producing an inadequate amount of artificial gasoline in factories, which were easily recognized by bombers because they were so big. One of these was located near the concentration camp of Auschwitz and was operated by starving prisoners. The inadequate supply of fuel from the very beginning of the War until its end, particularly as the War wore on and the situation became much worse, contributed to the defeat and fall of The Thousand Year Reich. Public restaurants, coffee shops and virtually all residences in Germany itself had hardly any fuel during the winter months. Only the big shots of the S. S., S. D., Gestapo had very well heated offices and facilities.

My boss, whom I knew from Rawa Ruska, explained that we would have to go by railway all the way, taking along all our heavy equipment, such as road building machinery, etc.

The Berlin office of the building firm Dr. Ing. W. Stickel was located in the fashionable district of Charlottenburg, not far from the famous Kurfuerstendamm.

On my first day in these luxurious quarters, one of the secretaries handed me a bunch of papers and told me that I would get the proper documentation and receive uniforms at the O. T. recruiting center on the outskirts of Berlin.

Wisely, I took along a small satchel containing black market items which I had brought all the way from Luck: several small bottles of good vodka, as well as some smoked sausage and bacon. Berliners were on very short rations, and I foresaw that these things would serve as welcome "gifts," (read "bribes").

After a horrendous night of bombing, I reported the following morning to the administrative offices of the O. T. As I passed through Berlin, houses were still in flames or smoldering, ambulances were trying to progress through the night's rubble, people were being carried around on stretchers, while others dug in the rubble.

I presented my papers and was transferred to the section of so-called "Auslaender," (foreigners). Different uniforms were issued for foreigners, usually black. Those for German nationals and so-called "Volks-Deutscher," who claimed German ancestry, were beige.

In the barracks where I was to be processed, I first came to a very old man who sat at a desk and asked me various questions. He was in charge of new arrivals and was obviously of high rank. Since I answered him in very good German, the interview proceeded on a very friendly basis, and he let me know that he could assist me in getting through all the formalities very fast. That was particularly welcome information, since Berlin was subjected to nightly air raids, which were infernal.

There were a tremendous number of bombs, howling sirens, raging fires. The fire brigades were unable to cope with the vast number of fire alarms, so buildings just burned and were destroyed. People ran into the basements of their homes or other air raid shelters on the average of 3 to 4 times a night. I certainly didn't want to stay too long at the barracks, which lacked shelters, other than little ditches. The O. T. induction center was quite a long way from the headquarters of the Firma Stickel in Charlottenburg, and I wanted to get back there rather than stay overnight in the barracks.

The old man told me that I would get processed up to a certain point that day, and then I should go back to my firm. This was also "irregular." I was to report again the following day at 5:00 A.M., a "wonderful privilege." I thanked him with some of my smoked ham, which he accepted very gratefully. This, of course, spurred him to do even more for me, hoping to receive some further goodies.

I had a very perfunctory medical examination. We had only to remove our shirts to be examined to see if our hearts were still beating. They looked at my eyes, ears, and mouth, and that was about it. Naturally, there were always very long waiting periods, where we sat around for hours awaiting the process. We were photographed and had to fill out some paperwork for our identity cards, and this was all that could be accomplished that first day.

    I reported back the following morning, and the old man immediately took me under his wing and shoved me over to the supply master. He talked with the guy a little, and then told me, "You just stick to my friend over here and he will supply you with a good uniform and good boots, warm clothing, which you will need when you go to Russia." "Nach dem Osten," (to the East) was always a word with dark significance to the Germans. East meant privation. It also meant the atrocities the Germans were conducting "out EAST!" That was where all the extermination camps were supposed to be. (Naturally, the concentration camps were all over Germany, but everyone noticed the transport of people in cattle cars, and they all went eastward! The actual extermination and burning in the crematoria and gassing of hundreds of thousands of people took place mostly in the occupied parts of Russia and Poland.) EAST was also frightening because that was where the German soldiers froze to death and were killed by the hundreds of thousands.

Naturally, I had to sign for every little piece of equipment -- every pair of socks, every handkerchief, every pair of underpants and so on. My "friend," the quartermaster, took me along and selected out all the best things for me. Of course, without saying, it was understood that he would receive a special "gift" from me; and I was prepared. He was overjoyed at the small bottle of good vodka, which I gave him. Berlin was virtually starving, and there were no luxuries.

He took away my black trousers and issued me some fine dark beige gabardine ones which obviously came out of the German officers department. All the way through, I got very good stuff, the best he could produce, and to my greatest surprise, I was officially issued a gun license and a brand new caliber 7.65 MM German Walther pistol and holster. I did not ask for it -- it was just given to me; and the old man told me that going where I was going -- "out EAST!" --
I might find I had very good use for it, and he wished me "lots of luck."

The issuance of the semi-automatic Walther pistol was totally illegal under German law, because no foreigner and especially no Pole could own such a German gun. However, once the paperwork was done, (and it was done without my initiative), and it was properly stamped and sealed, everything became totally legal. I had a weapon carrying permit!

During the proceedings I overheard a conversation between the chief of the processing center and one of his assistants that was both funny, but also politically significant. The assistant said, "But this man is a Pole!" (Meaning "untermensch" (subhuman). The chief said, "But he speaks good German." "Maybe he's a Volks-Deutscher (an ethnic German.") The chief said, "Who knows? 1st alles Schnuppe!" (Berlin dialect meaning "It's all the same.") "Maybe he thinks it might be better at the end of the War to be a Pole than a Volks-Deutscher." The implication, of course, was that the Allies regarded a Volks-Deutscher as a traitor to his home country, and as a matter of fact, many tens of thousands were thrown out of Czechoslovakia and Poland right after the War.

I parted from this recruiting center on very friendly terms with both the quartermaster and the commander. I gave them further foods, and they shook my hand and wished me good luck.

At the Stickel administrative offices I presented the credentials received at the equipping camp. I was handed a printed order (still in my possession) to report on 5 August 1943 to the O. T. unit in Krakow, Poland. I was utterly surprised.

I was told to get out of Berlin as quickly as possible because of the bombing. They would help me get organized and meet up with my Stickel unit. My boss, Mr. Makorov had left some days before.

    I had spent approximately a week in Berlin getting outfitted with credentials and clothing. The year was 1943, and the bombing was very heavy. On the way to and from the offices of Stickel the alarms went off regularly, particularly during the evenings and at night. I found myself in various basements and shelters. There I made the acquaintance of a young, very pretty student, a Berlin girl by the name of Heidi. We became very friendly and I invited her up to the Stickel apartments, which were quite luxurious. After 5:00 when the offices were empty, we spent some time up there listening to the radio and preparing meals. We had a rather torrid love affair and kept in touch for the next few months. I did not have any kind of permanent postal address, and when I wrote to her Berlin address, the house had been bombed and the postcard was returned. So, I lost track of my lovely friend.

    I was allowed to stay at the offices of the Firma Stickel, because with my "Polish" nationality, it would have been difficult for them to put me up in an hotel or pension. One had to declare one's nationality to the police and there were all kinds of sticky formalities involved. The offices occupied a whole floor in a patrician house in a very beautiful neighborhood in the section of Berlin known as Charlottenburg. It was located on the Giesebrecht Strasse 15, on the second floor. The offices consisted of eight to ten old-fashioned, very high-ceilinged, fancy and luxurious rooms, with a reception area and a service area, consisting of a very large tiled kitchen and two bathrooms. There wasn't a single bedroom, so I was told to sleep on a couch in the reception area. Early in the morning I straightened out everything so there was no trace of my having stayed there.

Dr. Ing. Wilhelm Stickel, a white haired gentleman, was an old-line party member, who wore a Nazi Party emblem on his lapel. He had two general managers, or Prokuristen. One of them I did not know at all. The other was a squat, rotund, half-bald man in his late 40's, Mr. Goerke. He gave orders to the various "bauleiters" (building site managers) such as Mr. Makarov. It was he who told me that the newest building site would be in Simferopol, which was on the Crimea. Mr. Makarov was to be the boss there, and he had requested that I should come with him. In addition there was a staff of secretaries and bookkeepers. I also became acquainted with Frau Weber, a widow in her 50's, whom I was to meet a year and a half later in Italy at one of the building sites. She was an extremely nice and friendly person.

At the Firma Stickel there was an old bookkeeper by the name of Walter, an old line Social Democrat. He openly cussed and swore at the Hitler regime -- what kind of pigs and bastards and murderers they were! Though I agreed with his thoughts, I was very uneasy because I felt that, under the circumstances he could be a provocateur. So I just nodded my head and made noncommittal sounds like, "Um Hmmm," etc. I did not want to get involved in any further discussion, especially in Berlin. It was too dangerous!

I was then about 19 years old, and I had lived through two of the most oppressive regimes of the 20th Century. First, I was in the eastern part of Poland, occupied by the Soviet Forces. That part of Poland was virtually run by the NKVD (the Soviet Secret Police). I was there as a foreigner, and we had to report to the NKVD on a monthly basis. The experiences I witnessed showed how merciless and arbitrary this dictatorial Stalinist regime was. People were murdered in cold blood in front of my eyes for no reason that I could discern -- except that they were not in agreement with the regime.

Thereafter, there was the occupation by the Germans. Of course, with my knowledge of languages, I felt all the nuances of the cruelty and repression that existed. There was also constantly the danger of being denounced; and denunciations took place on a grand scale. The Germans had large numbers of both Polish and Ukrainian collaborators. For an average American or average younger person in a civilized country to even imagine these conditions would be very difficult.

    I operated under a certain "haze" that enveloped the entire society -- a haze of deceit, secretiveness, and being constantly afraid and on the alert. In my particular position, with false papers and a false identity representing a person brought up in a different language and environment, I had to be extremely vigilant not to be detected. I was afraid of talking in my sleep. I had to be particularly attentive to small gestures such as the mode of eating, my way of talking to people. I had to be careful not to talk about remembrances of things past. It is difficult to try and paint an accurate picture of this appalling situation. I realize that the psychological burden placed upon me at that time has left an indelible mark on my personality.

    Leaving Berlin, I got on a train that went eastward. After many halts and stops (because of frequent bombing raids, and then approaching Poland the tracks were blown up by resistance groups and had to be repaired quickly before we could proceed), I arrived in Krakow after 3 or 4 days.

Once there I reported to the Stickel offices, which was again a small apartment in a rather nice residential part of the city. The manager, Miss Maria Hornych, allowed me to stay overnight. The next morning I met with my chief engineer, Mr. Makarov, as well as some of the other people who would also go to the eastern part of the Ukraine. Mr. Makarov was delighted when I came back properly dressed and fully equipped with belts and boots and gun, because he needed as good looking an assistant as he could possibly get, to use for various tasks of liaison with the German authorities. Mr. Makarov spoke somewhat accented German, whereby I had by then "learned" such good German that I spoke without any accent, which was of great advantage to him.

Makarov took me along with several German foremen to the train station where a freight train was already loaded with our equipment, such a bulldozers, road building equipment, 3 steam rollers. A caboose was provided as our "quarters" for the journey.

Mr. Makarov had an old Mercedes diesel passenger car, as well as a small BMW passenger car, obtained through some machinations with the O. T. We started off living in the caboose for the next month or so. We used the train station to provide us with food, water, and washing facilities. Other than that, we stayed on the train, which moved along extremely slowly. This train ride throughout the Ukraine would end up eventually in the main city of the Crimean peninsula, Simferopol. It was a long journey, interrupted constantly by halts, some for a day or two at a time. Again the railway tracks were blown up constantly, either by Russian bombing or by the partisans trying to interrupt the German supply routes.

We also waited while terrible trainloads of Jewish deportees, which had priority, passed us. It was one of those incredible actions of the Nazi regime that gave priority to the extermination camps and to the cattle cars in which they carried these poor people, rather than to the supplies of military equipment. Naturally, military trains also had precedence over our building materials or machinery trains.

The cattle cars filled with people were terrible to see and hear. One could hear them moaning or singing, begging for water or just crying out in fear, pain or despair. When such a train stopped, you could hear them, but it was strictly forbidden to go anywhere near these trains. They were closely guarded by troops with submachine guns slung around their necks, who would shoot if you approached.

We remarked from time to time about them, but mostly there was silence. To most of the Germans they were an embarrassment, and to elaborate on this subject was, of course, a grave political risk that could have serious consequences for anyone, including the Germans. We saw some people giving water or food to the deportees. On a couple of occasions I was able to throw some bread into the small openings of the cattle cars. They had barbed wire "X" crossed on them. People inside held out sticks with money fastened at the end. The guards chased the people around, and occasionally shot at them.

As we went through the Ukraine we saw some devastation. This was the end of spring/beginning of summer, and everything was green. We were even able to obtain some fresh fruit. Luxury!

Upon arrival in Simferopol, we started unloading all the equipment and were assigned to a barracks far out from the city, where we awaited further orders. Nothing happened! We sat there for several weeks doing absolutely nothing. During that time we made some interesting side trips "sightseeing." We visited several Moslem spas and Mosques, as well as the outskirts of Yalta.

I used the time with Mr. Makarov to visit Sewastopol, which was heavily bombed, both from the air and from a naval bombardment, and destroyed to a great degree; but it was still an interesting place to see. We saw only a small part of it - mostly cement bunkers. Still it was in a way exhilarating to be away from the terrible atmosphere of Lwow and the fear of someone recognizing my true identity and me.

Since I was able to converse in Russian or in Ukrainian with the local population, I found out that in November and December 1941, as well as in January and April 1942, all the Jews in Simferopol were murdered; and a similar massacre took place in the Crimean port of Kerch.

It is significant that in 1998, and 1999 a traveling exhibit in Germany showed the brutal participation of the German Army in the killings, massacres and tortures in the "East." Violent protests broke out in Hamburg, Munich, and Stuttgart by Neo-Nazis and rightists who wanted to perpetuate the myths that the Germany Army (Wehrmacht) was honorable and had nothing to do with war crimes and atrocities. At the Nuremberg trials, however, it was determined that Field Marshall Walther von Reichenau, commander of the German 6th Army, issued directives for the killings in the Crimea, which were also copied by General von Manstein. There was an "Order of the Day" of the 11th Army (20 November, 1941) to this effect. (International Military Tribunal, Nuremberg). I witnessed many instances of German Army units participating in the persecutions in the Ghettos and elsewhere. Today, after 50 years, the German rightists haven't got a foot to stand on. Nevertheless, public opinion in Germany is divided on this shameful and painful issue.

    Suddenly we received orders to load up all our equipment onto railway freight cars (without knowing at that point where we were going) to find out later on that we were going south and east. We did not understand what was involved. This was the crossing of the Straits of Kerch, which was the German Army's entrance to the Caucasus under the general command of General Paulus. General Paulus later surrendered his troops at Stalingrad, and was captured by the Russians; and later on started a German army on the Russian side.

    The transfer through the Straits of Kerch was upon military ferries, which used rubber boats and all kinds of other ferrying equipment. They got us across, and this whole operation took place during the night. It was totally black and we were not allowed to even speak or make any noise -- it was a very hush-hush operation. All the points of departure and landing on the other side were heavily guarded by military police.

On the other side in Kerch, we again got loaded onto railway wagons, and we kept on going in the direction of the Caucasus, but not very far. We stopped in the early morning between wheat fields and vineyards -- and stayed there for about two days, shunted aside. Nothing happened except for raids by small Russian planes that threw small bombs.

Through the grapevine we learned that we were overextended and could not get enough supplies over the Straits of Kerch. A couple of nights later, we were ordered to retreat, and wound up right back the same way we came -- only this time we got stuck in Kerch. And there we waited to be ferried across. While we waited, Kerch again came under heavy bombing by Russian planes. During one of the bombardments I was sent on an errand to some headquarters -- I don't recall the exact purpose -- but I do remember an air raid and bombs falling all over. I took a dive beside a small wall that saved my life. A bomb fell right on the other side and totally blew out one of my eardrums. I bled from that ear and couldn't hear out of the other one either.

The whole area was covered with dust from the many bombs, mostly smaller sized, presumably 50 to 100 Kg. After the raid I wanted to find a hospital or First Aid Station. I stumbled over many dead bodies and parts of bodies, such as arms and legs. Because of the cover of dust it was hard to distinguish what was lying around, broken pieces of pipe, auto parts, cement blocks, parts of buildings, broken glass.

Finally I found a near-by field hospital where they examined me and said, "Well, your eardrums are busted, but I guess they will grow together; and there's nothing we can do about it anyway, so keep on going." So I did. Finally we got shipped across the Strait of Kerch again in the dark of night, back to Simferopol and our former barracks. All our heavy machinery was left in Kerch, lost forever.

Unbeknownst to me and to the rest of us, the offensive on the Russian front took place and Hitler's armies advanced towards Stalingrad. We, of course, heard only about their victories. Again we were totally idle there and had nothing to do. Some of the machines that were left had to be repaired. Occasionally we went to Simferopol where there was a primitive movie house, where some German movies were shown in the evening. We used lightweight motorcycles to go back and forth.

After our return from the Kerch peninsula to Simferopol, we had the two cars, but no gasoline for the BMW, no mixture for the small motorcycles, nor diesel fuel for the Mercedes. Consequently, we were almost totally immobile because we had no access to fuel. So Mr. Makarov took me in the car (and this was on our last ten liters of diesel fuel) and told me that we would have to get some fuel. We loaded some empty gasoline canisters into our trunk and went off to a German Army supply depot. When we arrived there we asked where we would be able to get fuel, and we were directed to a sergeant who was in charge of diesel and gasoline. Because of the scarcity of fuel and the fact that the Crimea was cut off from the mainland, he had strict orders not to give out any type of fuel without the personal signature of the area Army General. At the present time they had no way of obtaining supplies, since the Black Sea was also a battle zone with the remnants of the Soviet Navy.

    Mr. Makarov requested an interview with the General. After we were shuffled past a lieutenant and then a major, finally we wound up in the anti-room of a large tent headquarters, where the General of the Crimea area had his office. The adjutant, also a major, asked our wishes. Mr. Makarov explained that we were cut off from our commanding headquarters and we didn't have any fuel. We had some highly important orders to fulfill, and we could not move because of the lack of fuel. We were told the only way to obtain any would be to have the personal signature of the General.

The adjutant disappeared, and finally we were asked to enter the General's office. We stood at attention, but Mr. Makarov made a big mistake. Instead of saluting, he gave the "Heil Hitler" salute with a raised hand. I had never seen Mr. Makarov give the Hitler salute except on this occasion. He was obviously desperate to obtain fuel. General "Freiherr von --------" became furious. He said, "We do not use this type of greeting at the front. This is a military zone, and we salute. There are no political expressions allowed in my area." He dressed Makarov down in a scream. Makarov stood in silence, and I took over and reported in short, telegraph style our situation, requesting permission to draw some fuel from the fuel depot for our purposes. The General told the Adjutant to give us documentation, and we were dismissed. Mr. Makarov all of a sudden remembered to salute properly, and we turned around and marched out of there. We got ourselves a half a barrel of diesel fuel.

The interesting part of this episode was the fact that the General was obviously of the old military school, and also obviously anti-Hitler and anti-Nazi. This was not the only experience I had with Germans in higher positions who were not in agreement with the regime. These manifestations were very dangerous to the Germans because the Gestapo had the last word.

It became obvious that the Russians had advanced against the German Armies and the access to the Crimea was cut off. It was also the time (it must have been November by then) that the big battle of Stalingrad took place. At that point Mr. Makarov got flight orders to report to Berlin, and I took him to the military airport in Simferopol.

I asked Mr. Makarov to try and get me out of there. More than anything else, I was very apprehensive staying with two principal foremen. They were very unpleasant characters -- low caste, uneducated, probably with criminal records. The worst, Gleichmann, a large, heavy-set man, was a tremendous bully. He disliked me particularly because I was a "damned Polak" heightened by the fact that I was an aide to Mr. Makarov. Makarov himself had no use for them because they were so stupid and crude. I stayed away from them as much as I could.

I had many difficulties with them, but I tried to keep calm, keep my head down and stay out of their way. Mr. Makarov shook my hand and told me, "I will try and see to it that you get marching orders to get out of here. There is nothing to do here anyway, because the Crimea is cut off; and maybe we can find a way to survive this war somehow." I was grateful and hopeful, though I knew I couldn't depend upon it.

I stayed on in those miserable barracks for weeks, until it turned into winter, which in the Crimea is very mild. After about a month and a half of sitting around, suddenly a messenger from the military O. T. headquarters in Simferopol came on a motorcycle, asking for the O. T. man "Chwistek." I knew something was up. He handed me an envelope containing my marching orders, including a flight order from Simferopol to Krakow. I was to report to the Krakow office of Stickel and the O. T. office there. I packed my things and without even saying good-by to those two characters (I was afraid to let them know I had received orders out, for fear they might try to kill me) I thumbed my way on a military truck to Simferopol and went with my little satchel on foot to the airport and presented my papers.

The German Army Sergeant who was in charge of sorting out and placing people on planes told me that I had better prepare myself for a long wait, because there were other people who had much higher priorities, such as officers, wounded soldiers. So I just camped out in front of the barracks of this Sergeant. I sat or walked around 3 or 4 days doing absolutely nothing, trying to keep myself as clean as I could at the local latrine. Finally one evening an assistant of the Sergeant said, "Come on! You can get on the next one." He guided me over to a Junkers Tri-Motor prop plane, and I hopped in. It was totally stripped inside. We all sat on the floor, and the thing took off with a great rattling and noise, and before I knew it, we were over the main Ukraine. We landed at night in the town of Winitsa, where I was told "that was it." and unceremoniously off loaded. They could take me no further because they had to take some seriously wounded soldiers and officers. Thus ended my first airplane ride!

    In the early morning hours I trekked over to the railway station and by hook or crook I got first onto a freight train, and later onto a passenger train. There were always long waits between trains. I stopped in Lwow and got off the train to visit my cousin, Olek. He worked as a bookkeeper in an electrical firm. He lived in a very small elongated room with just place enough for an iron bed, a small chifforobe table, and chair. It was miserably cold, and his place had no heat. I visited with him whenever I passed through Lwow, coming or going from the various building sites. We always spoke in whispers. I could not visit him more often, and did so on only a few occasions. I could not wear any kind of German uniform or part thereof. This would have made his landlord and neighbors suspicious. I had to change into my work clothes, and I did so, where else, in a dark alley. The visits were always after sunset when it was quite dark, as we had to be extremely careful not to expose him in any way.

    I left with him a heavily padded military type jacket, an O. T. issue. At first he was afraid to keep it, because it was German military property, but I convinced him that it was not regular army type. Fifty years later, during my visit to Poland in 1989, we had a fabulous dinner and get-together with him and his wife Joasia and their two married sons and their families. Suddenly he sprang up and brought the padded parka into the room and said, "I want to return this to you with my thanks. It helped me quite a bit during some cold nights." We all had a good laugh and I had a lot of explaining to do to my wife, Nancy.

    I finally made it into Krakow. I was glad to get there, to the bath in the Stickel offices, and a chance to get myself reorganized. I was told that Mr. Makarov had been dispatched from Berlin to our new building site in the vicinity of Udine, Italy, and I was to go there.

CHAPTER 19

ON TO ITALY

I was glad to get to Krakow, to the bath in the Stickel offices, and a chance to get myself reorganized. I was told that Mr. Makarov had been dispatched from Berlin to our new building site in the vicinity of Udine, Italy; and I was to go there.

Miss Hornych, the Stickel office manager in Krakow, Poland, who was also Mr. Makarov's girlfriend, saw to it that I got some up-to-date marching orders, helped me with some provisions, and put me on the train to Vienna.

I arrived in Vienna at the Ostbahnhof, and after staying overnight in Vienna and looking around in the city where I had spent my childhood, I went to the Sudbahnhof and boarded a military transport toward Tarvisio. There the German Military Police, as well as the Italian Military Police checked our papers. I had no problems. My "papers" were in perfect order!

I continued to Udine, where the mild climate and being away from all the horrors of war and the atrocities that I witnessed was an elating experience. I felt the greatest relief of all the tensions, and found Italy a haven and release from all the horrible happenings to which I was witness.

Mr. Makarov had quartered himself and the German staff in a beautiful villa, which was confiscated from a Jewish family in the little town of Buia, near Gemona. I was very grateful to Mr. Makarov, and he seemed happy to see me. I was quartered in a small room rented from an elderly family not far away from the Stickel headquarters. Makarow put me to work right away on many projects.

This was not only a very pleasant, but also a most interesting stay; although I had some frightening experiences there, too. We went into Udine for visits and stayed at the Hotel Croce de Malta. I was astounded that Italy had no food rationing. Everything was available -- all types of merchandise. It was paradise in comparison to the rest of Europe.

In the evening in Buia we had some nice get-togethers and had a few drinks of Vermouth Bianco in a nearby little bar, as well as in the offices of Stickel. Among the other secretaries, there was also Frau Weber, whom I had met and liked earlier in the headquarters of Berlin. She was also one happy person to get out from under the bombing raids and to be in Italy. She became acquainted with one of the local commanding officers of the Osopo Airport, Major Braun. Soon an obvious love affair developed between Frau

Weber and Major Braun, They joined us often for conversation and relaxation in the evenings.

On several occasions Major Braun explained how satisfied he was that he had been transferred from the Eastern Front to Italy. He had seen so many of the atrocities committed by German citizens, German police units, paramilitary units, and also by the German Army. He predicted that if the Allies won the War, which was already quite probable, the retribution against Germany and the Germans would be tremendous. Based upon the experiences of World War I, there would be mass executions and a terrible price to pay for the crimes committed by Germany.

Even to mention the fact that Germany might possibly lose the War was considered treason. There was only one penalty, and that was execution. Therefore, it was particularly enlightening to me that Major Braun would have the courage to express views that were shared by many, though few dared to speak them out loud.

During our stay in Buia, Mr. Makarov was called to high headquarters in the vicinity of Udine, and when he came back he indicated that this was a big hush-hush affair. He could not keep a secret anyhow, and soon he confided in me and showed me a booklet stolen by German espionage people from the American Sea-Bees. It was a technical method to transform soil mixed with cement and other ingredients into temporary runways for airplanes. The system was used extensively in the Pacific Theater of War. The booklet was translated from English into German, and we were supposed to use this method in making the runways for the jet fighters that were stationed in Osopo near our headquarters.

    The system worked to a certain extent, but after heavy rains the runways were not in usable condition. It was an interesting aspect to have insight into a booklet that was stolen by German spies from the Americans. (Disinformation?)

    We had some building contractors in Gemona who provided us with Italian forced laborers to make runways for the first jets flown by the Germans. They could stay in the air only about 5 to 10 minutes, and were supposed to shoot down American and English bombers as they came back to their southern Italian bases from air raids to Germany.

    I had many contacts, and I started speaking Italian, helped by my extensive studies of Latin for many years. My language experience at the Italian Command in Lwow also came in handy. In talking to people, when they found out I was not German, but Polish, they became very friendly. Basically, they were 98% anti-Nazi and anti-German.

They also introduced me to some rough looking men who turned out to be connected with the Italian partisans. They mainly operated out of the little city of Tarcento and Gorizia and the mountains around. It wasn't very long before I established connections and began helping these partisans at night to blow up the exit ramps for the airplanes that were hidden in holes in the mountains. The planes needed these ramps to get to the runways, and by blowing holes in the access strips, we prevented their getting out. They were locked in their holes in the mountains until the damage was repaired, in about 2 or 3 days.

Some nights I was awakened by detonations. Although my little room with an Italian family was about 2 Km. away from the Osoppo airfield, I knew that our dynamite (stolen from our Italian building contractors) had destroyed the approaches to the runways. Frightened people often ran out of their houses, thinking a bombing raid was occurring. I played my part, but laughed inwardly, rejoicing. The German airport command never let anything be known about the damage --- but we, "the Partisani" and I knew!

Although it was quite risky, I constantly removed dynamite and other explosive materiel -- blasting caps, and other paraphernalia, such as lightening wires -- from the magazines and put them into my little Fiat car. Then on my way back to the home base, I would drive very slowly and stop somewhere on the side of the road where there were bushes, where I had little hide-outs dug and covered with stones. Here I put all the materiel, then pretended to relieve myself. Afterwards I just kept on going.

I kept this up for several months. The amount of materiel I stole undetected was remarkable. However, the amount that I took out each time was of relatively small volume. Either no one noticed or the contractors did not want to notice, because this was too sensitive an issue. If they would have reported the disappearance of explosive materials, they would have gotten themselves into terrible trouble. So, I was able to supply the partisans with a lot of blasting materiel, which I know they used later on the railway and tunnels of the Tagliamento approaches into Italy.

My unit of the Partisans was located at Tarcento, which was a border village with Yugoslavia. The unit cooperated and was intertwined with the Yugoslav Partisans under the command of Marshall Tito.

One of the vital activities of our unit was to look out for downed British or American fliers. Some of the planes were damaged while bombing Germany, and came limping down toward their bases in Sicily, but had to be aborted. The aviators usually landed with their parachutes in the broad valley of the Tagliamento. It was one of our operational objectives to rescue these fliers and smuggle them into the territory that was held by the Tito Partisans. Some of these fliers were then transported on through eastern Europe to Persia (Iran). Persia, during the war was divided into two zones of influence: Soviet in the north, and the rest as an Anglo-American zone of influence. From there the pilots were sent back to southern Italy or Sicily.

We were constantly on the lookout for these men. Some of them were injured, and this was an additional problem. Although at the time it was not obvious to me, there were different groups of resistance fighters. Some of them were aligned with the Communists, and others with pre-war conservative parties. However, our units were closely connected with the resistance fighters of Yugoslavia which operated nearby and with the so-called Tito Partisans. I also had some contacts with operatives in the city of Udine, where I functioned as a courier to deliver and receive messages, most of which were coded. I observed that among the operatives of the resistance groups there were some British civilians who were obviously connected with the British spy apparatus. Shortly after I became involved with these groups the Italian military command was changed from British to American, and the American General Mark Clark took over the theater of war. I had my first contact with American operatives of the O.S.S. (the Office of Strategic Services,) which was the forerunner of the CIA. They were very astute and dedicated people who had good communications resources, radios and knowledge of local languages.

    Our activities intensified because the route from Germany to the Italian theater of war was supplied mainly on two roads and railway connections. One ran over the Brenner Pass, which was often bombed out of operation. The other one was over the Pass of Tarvisio in the Tagliamento. Although there was intensified bombing, it was not often hit because of the geographical and geophysical location of this railway and road, large portions of which ran through tunnels and were not even visible from the air. Consequently, the Partisans intensified the mining and blowing up of the railway tracks as well as planting explosive charges on some of the bridges of the highway. The Germans retaliated by intensifying their patrolling and also by terrorizing the local population in order to obtain information on our activities. In general our efforts were reasonably successful -- such as skirmishes with German patrols, which simply vanished and never came back to their bases.

All during this time I continued my job at the building site of Stickel, and I could participate in the actions of the partisans only during certain specified times. I could not stay away all night, which would have made my landlords suspicious, and that would have led subsequently to the police. In spite of this, I was able to do a lot of support and courier work for the partisan unit. With my small Fiat I was sent constantly on all kinds of errands. Nobody noticed that I did twice as many errands as I was officially asked to do. I was able to transport packages, most likely of explosives, to various locations, particularly into the direction of Pontebba, which was out toward the Austrian border and in the direction of Tarvisio.

I was particularly helpful with information on troop movements, since our building site was located very near the railway tracks, and I was able to note all the materiel and troop movements north and south on the Tarvis line. During my Sundays off, I managed to get away to do courier deliveries to Udine and other locations.

Then an extraordinary experience occurred. One beautiful spring day in 1944 Mr. Makarov sent me to the railway station in Gemona to pick up some packages. I went with one of our trucks and a driver. The railway station was oddly totally deserted, and I didn't even notice it -- just thought about it in retrospect. I went to the freight department and picked up the packages, threw them into the truck, and hopped in to return to our offices.

As we pulled out of the railway station and slowed down to cross the railroad line, two men in civilian clothes jumped onto the running boards of our truck, one on each side. The driver had enough presence of mind to push the man on his side away immediately. He fell off, and the driver stepped on the gas. The other guy hung on and produced an automatic pistol, which he started firing. As he fired, I opened my door and pushed him off. It was one of the partisans trying to kill us. The four fired bullets zipped by me and by my driver, chipping the steering wheel as well as some of the instruments of the truck; but we were spared serious injury save for a few scratches from the bakelite that flew around from the steering wheel. It was an irony that I so narrowly escaped death from the hands of an Ally. Although I later mentioned this incident to some of my liaison people in the partisans, no one remarked on this attack or assumed any responsibility.

Other than that, life was very pleasant around Udine.

AERIAL COMBAT OVER NORTHERN ITALY – AMERICAN BOMBERS, GERMAN PURSUIT PLANES 1944

LOOKING AT AERIAL COMBAT OVER NORTHERN ITALY 1944

MY FORMER BOSS IN LWOW ITALIAN HQ, SERGEANT LUIGI & WIFE, UDINE 1944

HEAVY BOMBARDMENT OF MONFALCONE, ITALIAN NAVAL SHIPYARDS 1944

DURING MONFALCONE BOMBARDMENT WE HID OUR CAR IN A TUNNEL 1944

VIEW OF RAIL & & HIGHWAY OVER THE TAGLIAMENTO RIVER, GERMAN SUPPLY ROUTE 1944

BUILDING FIRM STICKEL HQ IN ITALY NEAR UDINE 1944

PICKING UP OFFICE MACHINES IN SIRMIONE 1944

STICKEL WORK ASSEMBLY SITE FOR CONSTRUCTION OF RUNWAYS & TUNNELS FOR GERMAN JET FIGHTERS, OSOPPO, ITALY 1944

RUNWAY CONSTRUCTION WORKSITE FOR FIRST GERMAN JET PURSUIT PLANES 1944

**FIAT CAR ASSIGNED TO ME
I USED IT TO TRANSPORT SABOTAGE MATERIEL
1944**

CHAPTER 20

ZAKOPANE

The Building firm Stickel had offices coordinating the Eastern European building sites in Krakow, Poland. They rented a nice apartment on a side street in the downtown area. Krakow, for reasons of historical treasures, had been spared from bombing. There was very little damage to the city.

The office consisted of a good-sized apartment with three bedrooms, kitchen, a small bathroom, living room and dining room. The living room and dining room were converted into offices. Miss Hornych, who was the chief of this office and its only permanent employee, occupied one of the bedrooms. The other two bedrooms were just for visitors passing through Krakow to the various building sites in Poland, Ukraine, Byelorussia, and the Crimea.

For me the stay in Krakow was always a great relief from the hardships of some of the building sites.

On one occasion Miss Hornych was away for a couple of days while I had to wait for some traveling papers to arrive. She asked me to answer the phone for her and take in the mail and stack it on her desk. Other than that, I had no responsibilities.

A Polish cleaning woman came every day to straighten out the apartment. Since I spoke Polish, she engaged me in conversation. She asked if I knew how to ski, to which I replied, "Yes, I do." She said, "I want you to meet two young ladies who work for the railroad administration here in Krakow. I also work as a cleaning woman for them in their apartment. The railway gives them coupons to go skiing to Zakopane in the nearby Polish Tatra Mountains, but they don't like to go alone. They are looking for a male companion who knows how to ski to go with them. If you want, I'll put you in touch with them."

I, naturally, was very happy to go for a couple of days to Zakopane, especially since I wouldn't otherwise have this opportunity. I received their phone call, and was soon on my way to meet two very lovely young women. One, whose name was Annaliese, was from northern Westphalia, and the other, by the name of Linda, from the area of Stuttgart. Both had railway passes, as well as vouchers to stay at a bed and breakfast in the famous resort town of Zakopane. We met on a Thursday, and on Friday evening we met again at the railway station; and off we went on our weekend ski trip.

The two ladies had their own ski equipment, but I rented mine at the cable car station in Zakopane. The ladies had all the necessary coupons and vouchers for the various facilities. Everything was very companionable and we had a very sunny and beautiful skiing weekend.

Both of the ladies were tremendous flirts and seemed to compete to attract me. Annaliese was married, but she had not heard from her husband in over a year, since he was sent to the eastern front. Over the next few months we kept in touch, writing cards and letters. Annaliese could obtain railway tickets whenever and to wherever she wanted, and was able to come wherever I was to visit with me.

Even in the beauty and freedom of skiing in the Tatra mountains with delightful company, I was haunted every day with thoughts of the heartbreak and hardships my parents experienced, and our eventual separation and their terrible, torturous deaths. These memories have accompanied my entire life. A day rarely passes without some flashback in my imagination, comparing my activities and well being with the heartbreaking persecutions we all went though during the War years.

Shortly after we met, Annaliese and I began a love affair. We got along very well, and we were both very much in love with one another. It was unusual and remarkable that in the very beginning of our more intimate relationship, she mentioned the fact that her grandparents "disappeared" a couple of years ago. To disappear in Nazi Germany meant only one of two things: either you were Jewish, or you were politically opposed to the regime. There was never a clear explanation from her about the possible cause of their disappearance. It was almost obvious to me that they must have been either Jewish or half-Jewish, and that was the reason they were arrested by the Gestapo, and no one every heard from or saw them again.

It was symptomatic of the conditions of Nazi Germany that, even among married people or boyfriend and girlfriend, communication and conversation was very constricted and limited. Fright that one might be overheard, or some harmful information might slip out inadvertently always lurked in the atmosphere. This behavior can be appreciated and understood only if you can imagine the tremendous pressures of police surveillance and repression that exists in dictatorial regimes, such as Nazi Germany or Stalinist Russia.

Annaliese came to visit me when I was in northern Italy for periods of two or three days at a time. Also when I traveled with Mr. Makarow on business trips to Prague, she met us in Vienna and traveled on with us to Prague on the railroad.

In the latter part of 1944, when the Soviets moved westward and the Red Army occupied Krakow, I realized that Annaliese was probably evacuated further west, possibly into Germany. However, in spite of the fact that Annaliese had my address, I never received another message, letter, or word from her.

At the end of the war I undertook to try to locate her, but without success. I must surmise that in the war-torn turmoil and evacuation of Krakow, she must have perished, as so many people did. It is always very dangerous and chaotic when the various armies move forward and the others withdraw.

This was also the worry of Mr. Makarow in Italy. He thought the movement of the fronts of the allies northward and the withdrawal of the Germans would be one of the most dangerous times that we had to face. Consequently he decided to move into the mountains of Austria. There in relative obscurity, he hoped to avoid being caught between the two fronts.

CHAPTER 21

THE SILVER TRIP

After having lived for almost 3 years in German occupied Poland and Russia, the atmosphere in Italy was overwhelmingly pleasant. Not only was the climate very benign, but the people were all very well dressed, and to our eyes, very elegant looking. Even in conversation, the difference was enormous. People talked like during peacetime. They were preoccupied with cooking, entertainment and shopping.

In the eastern parts of Europe, there were no window displays, and very few stores functioned. While traveling through Germany and Austria the situation was somewhat better, but there was a tremendous scarcity of items that one could buy because there was total price control. Naturally, under such conditions, the black market was very active. However, that did not change the overall looks of a city or village. The black market did not display their goods.

In Italy the conditions were almost like pre-war. Sporting goods stores offered all types of sports equipment, clothing stores displayed fashionable goods. Most women bought materials, of which there was a very large selection, to have seamstresses make their dresses and coats; and I noticed also that gentlemen bought fine English worsted materials by the meter and had tailors fashion their good looking suits.

    We were in awe, confronted with a different economy. The Italians complained about high prices, because they suffered from considerable inflation; but this did not register with us, since their prices were still approximately the same as we had to pay pre-war. The only problem was that we did not have enough money. Every employee in our firm wished to buy all kinds of things, but did not have the means. Some of our German employees wanted to buy food parcels and send them back to relatives in Germany. Mr. Makarov needed to buy clothing for his wife as well as for his small child. I wanted to acquire a good set of skis and ski boots, because the mountains were near, and I figured that sooner or later I might be able to use them.

    After some extensive "market research" I found out that the jewelers with whom I spoke in Udine were anxious to purchase silver, in any form. Their artisanship in creating silver jewelry and artifacts was renown, but they lacked the raw material. No one in Italy at that time wanted to part with either gold or silver, and therefore, the black market price of these metals was sky high.

    After talking my plans over with Mr. Makarov, we put together a sizable "kitty" of whatever Reichsmarks we could lay our hands on, and Mr. Makarov produced military marching orders for me from Udine to Krakow, Poland via Vienna and on to Warsaw and return. All this was on "urgent Firma Stickel "Org. Todt" business." The official purpose of this trip did not exist.

    I took off with two suitcases, one inside of the other. I changed trains in Vienna and went on to Krakow. I passed easily through the many police, M. Ps., railroad police, and even civilian Gestapo controls with these good "military marching orders." I stayed overnight at the Stickel offices in Krakow. This was convenient because thus I evaded the necessary registration with the police. I continued on to Warsaw, where I went straight to the soldier's home for transients near the railway station, checked in there with the same marching orders, and proceeded into the city in civilian clothes. I went from pawnshop to pawnshop and bought up all the silver cutlery I could. I immediately removed all the blades from the knives, since I was interested only in the silver handles, as well as the spoons and forks. I was able to buy this scrap silver by the Kilo at very favorable prices. It did not matter whether it was 900 proof or Sterling, or 800 proof. I bought whatever they had. The payment in Reichsmarks was illegal in occupied Poland. The legal currency was German script. Consequently,

Reichsmarks were desirable because they represented a "real" currency, and not just a bunch of fake paper.

    Returning to my quarters, I stashed all this silver wrapped in newspapers into the smaller of my two suitcases. Within two days I had amassed approximately 15 Kilograms of scrap silver. There was still room left in my small suitcase. I went to the railway station to board a train to Krakow. I waited until a new train rolled into the station and boarded. The compartments were empty. I put my extremely heavy suitcase on a luggage rack in one compartment, and continued with my second suitcase into the next wagon. This way, in case of a control, I was in no way connected with the illegal silver. The risk involved with this procedure was clearly discussed and understood by all my "stock holders."

    In Krakow, I was very slow in leaving and waited until the compartment where my silver suitcase was emptied. Then I picked up my other suitcase and walked back to Firma Stickel. I continued my round to the various pawn shops and "used" stores buying up an additional amount of silver to fill my suitcase. My sturdy leather suitcase with two straps around it now weighed approximately 20 Kilograms (44 pounds). I caught the next available train via Vienna to Udine, using the same system so as to avoid being associated with this contraband. Crossing four borders -- General Government (Poland), to Czechoslovakia, through Germany (Austria) into Italy -- there were border inspections at each crossing. The inspection was centered mainly on personal papers such as passports, marching orders, etc. There was no luggage control in the limited time available to the police.

In Udine Mr. Makarov picked me up from the railway station with his car (I had called from Vienna) and the next week I was very busy negotiating, selling, and distributing profits. This was my early training as a salesman. A friendly jeweler on the main street, Vittorio Emanuele, in Udine, bought the major portion of the silver. The division of the spoils was a happy occasion in the main office of Stickel in Buia at night. Since at that time the 5000 and 10,000 Lire banknotes were extremely large, some of us had to fill a shoebox full of banknotes. This money carried us through the rest of the war, and in fact, Mr. Makarov and I exchanged some of it back into Reichsmarks when we started building our little barrack in Austria.

Years after the war upon my visit to Udine I again ran into my friendly jeweler, who embraced me, kissed me on both cheeks, and invited me to a fine dinner. Obviously he must have made out well with the silver. He was probably the best supplied jeweler in all of northern Italy at the time.

He sold a lot of his production to Venice, where even during the war, the tourist trade never diminished. Venice was an open city, German military personnel could enter, but only unarmed.

Not long after this escapade, Mr. Makarov was called to Trieste. Since he did not like to travel alone, I was ordered to be the driver. On our way back, we stopped for a day in Venice, but a short way out of Trieste, in the morning hours of a beautiful day with blue skies, we heard the rumblings of a large formation of Allied bombers. We were well trained to recognize the sounds. I pulled the car into one of many tunnels on the road between Trieste and Venice, and we just sat down on the hillside. We witnessed the total destruction of the Italian shipyards and submarine base at Monfalcone and bombardment of the city. I had my little Leica with me, and I have the pictures still today in one of my albums.

An hour later, we went on to Venice where I spent the first of many glorious visits to that magical city.

CHAPTER 22

THE WAR ENDS......

The war was winding down and it was obvious as we got into 1944 that Germany would lose. Mr. Makarov was apprehensive and preoccupied about how to survive the end of the war. He said that the end of the war would be the most dangerous time for all of us (little did he know). He took to traveling and was gone anywhere from 3 days to two weeks. Later in 1944 he told me that he wanted me to go with him to establish a new base in the Austrian Alps, where Stickel would have a new building site under his direction.

We went on the train to Bad Ischl, the resort town where I had spent a summer vacation with my parents in 1934. He had already made the acquaintance of a forester in the government forestry department. He had prepared all kinds of documents on Stickel stationery about starting a building site. It became obvious that the whole thing was an elaborate ruse and scheme for Mr. Makarov to avoid getting involved in any kind of war action in Udine, which he anticipated as probable with the Allies moving up the boot of Italy.

Through bribery he obtained a small parcel of land called the <u>Hubhanslau</u> from the forester. It was beside a little creek and pretty barren. We returned to Udine and started assembling a whole barrack, getting a railway car to transport it, and recruited one Italian worker, a rough carpenter. He was a very handy man, to whom Makarov promised good pay and a demijohn of wine (because he wouldn't work without a little wine every day). We took along as many tools and supplies as possible, such as roofing rolls and shingles, wood and 2 X 4's, some sacks of cement, plywood, a stove, electrical materials, etc. Then off we went with our barrack and freight car without good-byes to anyone. The freight car was shunted back and forth, and it took 10 days before we finally arrived in Bad Ischl, Austria (then Germany).

We made arrangements with a freight forwarder to get the wagon unloaded. This was primarily my job, since Mr. Makarov was busy with paperwork, documentation, and the local authorities. Since the parcel of land had no access by road -- only walking paths -- we had to construct a rope pulley to ferry all the barrack parts and the appliances, furniture, etc. across the creek. We stayed at a hotel and did this work mostly at night. In the morning we started to put together the foundations, and I was the one who had to go to the hardware stores, building yards, and chisel out all the necessities. Fortunately, we had plenty of gravel and sand right there in the creek bed, so we laid the foundations in a hurry and got the barrack up. The place got built and the weather got cold, and soon after we had the roof on, our Italian disappeared into thin air. He just wanted to go home and didn't want to tell us because he was concerned that Mr. Makarov would probably try and keep him there. We finished as much as we could ourselves, for there was no labor available for help. Later Mr. Makarov contracted with a nearby small prisoner of war camp for some French soldiers for help. One of them promptly shacked up with the lady next door, and was never seen again, he spent all his time with her.

Thus we found ourselves in late 1944 in Bad Ischl. I was sent from time to time with fake marching orders to scrounge up bread and travel provisions. I would go by railway to Salzburg, Linz, Attnang-Puchheim, etc. to get all the provisions I could on the marching orders, which had attached coupons. Mr. Makarov also brought his wife and little daughter from his wife's home in Braunschweig.

On the 6th of May 1945 a jeep with American soldiers pulled into the main church square of Bad Ischl. I was there, and stepped forward to talk with the soldiers of this patrol. They had come on the western road to Bad Ischl from the direction of Salzburg. I told them about a division of Waffen S. S. camped in the woods of the Weissenbach Tal and the next crossroads to the east, between the River Ischl and the Lake Attersee. I thought this information might be important to them, and they should forward it to their headquarters. They did so immediately by radio. I found out later that the U. S. forces sealed off that valley from both the north and south ends. The Waffen S. S. regiment commanded by an S. S. General surrendered without a fight, showed a white flag, came out with their hands behind their heads, and were taken as prisoners of war. All their materiel was also carted off.

     In this chaotic aftermath of the War, I tried to re-establish my true identity. This took months, because there were no postal or telephone services. Austria was divided among the four victorious powers, and luckily I found myself in the American sector. I turned in all my documents to the local Austrian authorities. They were not too well organized as yet, but eventually various documents that still existed in the communal offices and the police headquarters in Vienna arrived, and I once again became "Heinz Gleisner."

Shortly after the Americans marched into this part of the country, out of nowhere appeared the so-called "Resistance Fighters." They all had red-white-red armbands, and declared themselves as a political organization, which had functioned underground. I had been in Austria for the last year of the war, and I can assert that I had not discerned even a <u>whiff</u> of any kind of resistance activity. Certain Austrians had been arrested and sent into the concentration camps, but these were usually political figures from pre-war times, who were known opponents of the Nazis. Now, all of a sudden, there seems to have been a lot of Austrian "resistance and opposition." I didn't believe it then, and even less so now.

A few days after the arrival of the American troops in Bad Ischl, Austria, I contacted the officials of both the Military Government and the new Austrian administration. Ing. Kragora, an Austrian engineer of the old school, who was kind and intelligent, was running the labor office. I was assigned many different tasks by this labor office, but one of the first things I wanted to do was to care for the victims of the Ebensee concentration camp. Two of the cruelest camps of the administration of the Hitlerian S.S., Ebensee and Mauthausen (a stone quarry) were near Bad Ischl. Those who survived Ebensee were veritable walking, living corpses, and had to be carried out on stretchers.

Bad Ischl boasted some superb hospital facilities for German soldiers injured in the War, complete with surgery for head injuries and other specialties. These hospitals were in top notch condition, Bad Ischl having been a Spa for centuries. Upon approaching the German doctors on behalf of a group of concentration camp victims, we found that there was a combination of fright and passive resistance. The American military governor of this section was Captain O'Keefe from the State of New York. He did not speak German but when I informed him of these facts, he dispatched military police to the German doctors, who were given two hours to clear the wards for the victims who had survived Ebensee. In spite of this, we lost many of the inmates because they were beyond medical help. The time factor was crucial in rescuing these wretched remnants of humanity. In many cases they were stacked in big piles, and we could not tell who was still alive or who was already dead. They all had been starved to death or nearly so.

We did not let the German Air Force (Luftwaffe) doctors near them. U. S. medical personnel, and shortly thereafter UNRRA (United Nations Relief and Rehabilitation) people took charge.

In the concentration camp there was a large pile of naked, dead bodies, which had to be buried in mass graves dug by bulldozers. The prisoners had killed a few of the guards before their liberation, but most of them had either fled or been taken prisoner.

I started to work for the American Military Government. One of my first suggestions was that the local cinema should show films of the U. S. Army liberation of the concentration camps. All officials of the local government, as well as many prominent citizens, were "invited" to view these films. Their uniform reaction was one of total silence. It was impossible to make comments upon the horrors that were shown. Of course, they had proof of everything right in their own little town. Denial of the Holocaust is one of the worst characteristics of defending a regime of horror, torture, and war crimes -- a most contentious state, worse than lies.

The Military Government assigned a local hotel, Hotel Weisses Kreuz, for the survivors, who lived there for a while. They immediately created a Jewish Community Council, and I was elected a member. I have the certification until today with my picture and a stamp with the "Mogan David." I helped to make sure that they had provisions and proper clothing, and food,. I made the acquaintance of an American lawyer from

Chicago, Mr. Gelber, who was working for the Property Control in Linz, Austria. His commanding officer in the American Military Government was Mr. B. G. Loehner, who was trying to establish legitimate rights to confiscated property, not only of Jews but also of other political opponents of the Nazi regime. One of the expropriated properties was the "Villa Felicitas" (the famous "Schratt Villa" given by Emperor Franz Josef to his lover, Maria Schratt) in Bad Ischl. It was an irony that I found myself assigned administrator and was also given living quarters in this historical Villa in 1945.

    The villa was quite sizable and the whole upper floor was assigned to me. There was much more room than my fiancée and I could use, so I invited one of the survivors of the Ebensee Concentration Camp, with whom I had worked on the committee to supply the survivors at the Hotel Weisses Kreuz. Thus Ted K. moved into an extra room on the other side of the entrance hallway, which was quite large. Soon thereafter he got involved with a young German actress. Their lovemaking was quite noisy and contributed to some amusement for us. It was remarkable that most people, whether Austrian or the survivors, seemed to become very active sexually immediately after the end of the War. It was a psychological reaction to the tremendous amount of loss of life that the war had caused. I can not explain it in any other terms.

Since the income from the various jobs I took on was very limited, I naturally got involved in some of the black marketing. In those days, the black marketing was actually the true market, because a free market did not exist. There were regulated food sales at unrealistically low prices that were based upon coupons, which were given out by the township offices, but these were insufficient to live on. The most common commodity of the black market was cigarettes. There were very stringent regulations. You could not slaughter a young piglet, because that would be less efficient than letting it grow up to have more meat for distribution. Some of the farmers around Ischl offered young pigs at very high prices, and this was another black market commodity, since in Austria this meat dish was very desirable and popular. We had a small slaughtered pig up in our apartment on the 2nd floor, when some gendarmes entered downstairs to make a surprise inspection. It was in the middle of the winter, so I opened the window and pitched the little piglet way out into the snow. It was a flying pig. After the gendarmes had left, we went out into the snow covered field and retrieved the little pig to be sold the next day.

A lot of the profits I made on the black market went to help the survivors of the Ebensee concentration camp, who were living in Bad Ischl. It was not a very pleasant life for the survivors. The Austrian population whispered about their being freed criminals. There was even a small group of Ukrainians I helped, because the Jewish survivors explained to me that they had been very decent, and protected them from being murdered by the guards in the final days of concentration camp.

We also heard from many other survivors that they were actually kept in the same barracks where they had been imprisoned by the Nazis; but this time they were guarded by American M. P's, and still could not leave the camps. I read in the newspapers that when President Truman found out about the poor treatment of the survivors, he intervened with General Eisenhower "to look into the situation!" After that the conditions improved greatly. American Military Government found better locations for the survivors to live until they could find a country to which to emigrate.

The majority of the survivors, of course, wanted to go to Palestine; but the British government refused to accept them. The situation was exceedingly difficult. Zionists representatives clandestinely assembled groups for transport from Austria to Italy, and from the Italian ports thereafter to Palestine. This created several tragic situations, that were well documented and even made into movies and books about the Exodus ship and others. It was a time of turmoil and chaos. Millions of people were moving east to west and west to east as refugees and displaced persons.

People waited in various displaced persons camps for visas and documents to settle in Canada, Australia, New Zealand, Central America, and the United States.

Finally I received an affidavit from my relatives in Detroit. They were very good people, but bore great guilt feelings, evident in their letters. They were interested in my coming as quickly as possible to the United States. My entry visa was greatly facilitated by my service in Italy, as well as my work for the American Military Government in Austria. But the fact remains that the lack of an affidavit, while my family was in the Soviet occupation zone of Poland in Lwow, was a disaster for us and a contributing factor to the deaths of my parents. Had we been able to escape at that time, my parents would probably have survived the War.

There were several Jewish and other organizations that tried to help some of the displaced persons. The organization I remember best was the Joint Distribution Committee that facilitated my communications with my distant family in Detroit. They also introduced me to the American Consulate in Munich, where my papers were processed. I went there several times to check on the progress of my travel documents, and I was treated extremely well. Many of the other people who wanted to emigrate to the United States had to wait years.

THIS IS NOT A TRAVEL PERMIT
KEINE REISEBESCHEINIGUNG

Registration-Certificate
Registrierungsbescheinigung
No.

Chairmann — Vorsitzender

Committee — Komitee

Date:
Datum: 18.1.46

The bearer is a Displaced Person and is registred by his National Committee in Linz.
Der (Die) Inhaber(in) ist eine Displaced Person und ist von seinem (ihrem) nationalen Komitee in Linz registriert.

DISPLACED PERSONS REGISTRATION

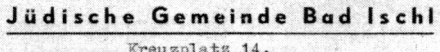

MEMBER IDENTITY CARD AS A BOARD OF DIRECTORS OF THE JEWISH COMMUNITY IN BAD ISCHL, AUSTRIA, 1945

CHAPTER 23

THE ULTIMATE CORRUPTION OF THE NAZIS

It was said about Joseph Goebbels Nazi propaganda machine, that if you repeat a lie often enough, some people would believe it. In the case of Nazi Germany, this was more than true. In the late '30's the followers of Hitler tried to picture themselves as honest, upright, "good Germans." They wished only to restore Germany to its rightful place and preserve the purity of the German race. The implication was that they would never tolerate dishonesty, corruption, and thievery.

In my extensive experience the Nazi system consisted for the most part of corruption, dishonesty, and thievery.

The corruption was exacerbated by shortages of almost all material things: food, clothing, gasoline, oil, coal, and luxury items. It was obvious to virtually all Germans at the time that the ordinary people faced shortages, while the Nazi elite, the so-called "Bonzen" not only enjoyed luxuries, but also enriched themselves immensely by stealing property and money from the people the regime persecuted. All postwar denials notwithstanding, this was common knowledge and was discussed and joked about on a daily basis. The same pertained to the existence of the so-called K.Z., the concentration camps. There was no secrecy about Dachau, Buchenwald, Mauthausen, Bergen-Belsen, etc. In fact, the K.Z. entered common conversations, such as "Watch out that they don't catch you and put you into the K.Z."

    The prevailing atmosphere of corruption was all encompassing. The illegal acquiring of goods even had an ironic name: "Organisieren." Since I was always the low man at the company offices, I was sent out routinely to "organize" special foods, fuel, chocolate, tools, building materials, just to name a few items. Because I was able to function on several levels, both as to language and social and national levels, I became successful at the tasks assigned to me. This in turn provided me with certain advantages. I was able to obtain better living quarters, better treatment, and the discriminatory practices against Poles were decidedly muted in my case. It is important to remember that I functioned as a Pole. It got me out of the Crimea that was cut off by the Red Army advancing toward Odessa.

    One of my cousins, Mr. Janek Brumer, was caught engaging in underground anti-German activities in Krakow. He was dispatch on two occasions to the concentration camp at Auschwitz, and each time his parents bought back his freedom by bribing some S.S. concentration camp guards. It must be remembered, however, that both he and his parents were considered Poles, and not Jews. In the case of Jews it would have been nearly impossible to free him, because of the certain death penalty that would have been meted out in such a case.

  The atmosphere of corruption influenced also the functioning of the so-called "Judenrat," the Council of Jews in the Ghettos. Although I spent only a short time in the Lwow Ghetto I became quite familiar with the functioning and tribulations. The German S.S. officers would visit the Council and leave orders to provide a large sum of money or to provide a large number of "workers" within a short time to be shipped out to factories important to the war effort. In each case the Jewish Council deluded itself into hoping to save their people, in spite of obvious evidence to the contrary. This dilemma manifested itself very visibly in the questionable activities of the Jewish Ghetto Police. In the end they were all executed anyway.

  As I described previously, I used a low level type of bribery at the Berlin headquarters of the Organisation Todt. I used the same methods whenever I was ordered to provide goods and services that were impossible to obtain otherwise.

Some people have asked me whether I feel that I "won" my personal war against Nazi Germany. I do not think so. In spite of the fact that I escaped with my own life, I was rendered totally powerless to rescue most of my family, and above all, my parents. I have not been able to escape a certain psychology of guilt feelings. After reading many of the accounts of the Holocaust, I understand that this is a common amongst almost all survivors. The most important part of my survival make-up at the time was that I trained myself that under no circumstances did I want to be a victim. I never let that thought even enter consciousness. To the contrary, I took pains to try and get even. And in a small way, I succeeded. But not enough!

    Shortly after the end of the war and after I had served at the American Military Government in Austria, I became for a short while a ski instructor for American G.I's in the Bavarian Alps. My students were U. S. soldiers of every rank. We generally had a very pleasant time, involving a lot of beer and schnapps drinking. One of the most popular games was "graduating" the class. We took the Zugspitz Bahn all the way to the top and admired the beautiful view. On our way back, when the little keg railroad came out of the tunnel, we asked the conductor to halt it a few seconds. Everyone of the class jumped out of the train with their ski equipment, secured their skis to their boots, and started skiing down as best they could to the village of Garmisch. The man who arrived last had to pay for the evening's drinks. Consequently, we celebrated every night!

Afterwards, I became active in helping my wife to establish a dental facility at UNRRA an camp for refugees, mostly concentration camp survivors. I traveled to Munich, Bamberg, and Nuremberg to obtain needed dental supplies. The Nuremberg War Crimes Court was in session. I tried to attend, but was unable to do so.

After the war, having had much to do with the "Denazification processes," I constantly met with denial and was told: "They didn't know; there were good sides to Hitler and Nazism, not only bad sides; that the German Army was honorable and honest; those atrocities and things that were reported were lies and didn't really happen." When I visited cities such as Munich, Nuremberg, and Berlin, and saw the total destruction of once proud historical buildings as heaps of rubble on the ground, and the streets as narrow pathways between those heaps of rubble, although they told of enormous suffering of the German people, I had difficulty summoning up any sympathy. Rather, I had to beat down the feeling that they got what they had coming!

Poverty, malnutrition and the loss of family and loved ones, both soldiers at the front as well as victims of the bombings were a burden that the German people had to bear. Millions of homes and apartments had vanished. How many were buried in the rubble?

Nevertheless, the returning or displaced victims of their criminal government were still treated atrociously. Having seen first hand the injustice, suffering, torture, mass killings, and horrible deaths dealt out by their agents, I could not feel for their suffering. They had life.

Reflecting later on, I also became critically aware of the inaction of the western governments, and last, but not least, of American Jewry.

CHAPTER 24

CAREER ON HOLD

As a young high school student, I had some firm ideas about my future. I wanted to become a motion picture director. Since my family was involved in the motion picture industry, they were quite agreeable to my idea, and had planned, upon my graduation, to send me over to England to a cinematography school that specialized in educating cinematographers of all kinds: technicians, photographers, directors; and in an adjoining school, also actors.

Naturally, nothing came of my plans. Instead we became refugees, and I became a Ghetto Jew with an armband with the Star of David. From there, I graduated to become a Polish slave laborer. As time passed, I worked myself up to a position of an accepted Pole (only subhuman). That enabled me to become active in the resistance later working with the Italian Partisans.

After liberation in 1945, I went with other young people skiing in the mountains of Bad Ischl. I started dating a local dentist, Yvette Kellner. Since there were very few cable cars, we often met on Friday evening and climbed all during the night to the high lying snowfields. We stayed in small mountain refuge huts and skied Saturday and

Sunday. When I think back I cannot imagine where we got the stamina and strength to climb all those mountains, walking uphill for several hours with artificial fur strips buckled onto our skis, a rucksack on our backs.

In 1946 Yvette and I were married in Bad Ischl, and lived for a time in the famous Schratt Villa. Since I was involved in the rehabilitation of some of the concentration camp victims, we became acquainted with a Ukrainian survivor, Mike Sobara. Eventually, after we got established in Michigan, we helped him immigrate into the United States. He joined us in Saginaw, where we lived and worked at that time. He had married a German woman who had a son from a previous marriage. They had three girls, making a happy, large family.

I remember Mike trying to secure some gasoline for me in Bad Ischl. He proudly brought me two military canisters full. It turned out that they contained only water rather than gasoline. Luckily I had not poured it into the car before discovering it. The black market had some pitfalls.

During our stay at the UNRRA displaced persons camp near Bamberg, Yvette established a dental station. It was a very busy place, because the survivors of the concentration camps, slave laborers and other refugees had received no dental care for years. Yvette became pregnant and our travel documents arrived. We arrived in the United States penniless and expecting our first child. Two months after our arrival, our daughter Karin Elisabeth was born at Harper Hospital in Detroit, Michigan. I started working on the automotive assembly lines in Detroit, and again tried to work my way up. After a while I used my previous experience to become a ski instructor in Michigan -- one of the first.

In 1951, our second child, Eric Kim was born also at Harper Hospital.

Later on I became a buyer for a wholesale sporting goods firm and in the 1950's I founded my own importing and exporting firm, St. Lawrence Sales, which was primarily active in the ski business at first, and later in the equestrian field. Times were hard! It was difficult starting a new business. I worked long hours and traveled selling, and had little time at home with my family.

Eventually Yvette became dissatisfied with her life. She was unable to continue her practice of dentistry in the United States because the requirements were so stringent. In 1961 we were divorced and she returned to Germany to resume her dental practice.

After thirty years in the import/export business I received the prestigious "E" Award" for excellence in exporting from the Department of Commerce, from then Secretary of Commerce

Mossbacher, in a ceremony in Washington, D.C. There followed a ceremony in Lake Orion, Michigan, where then Congressman Broomfield presented me with a certificate of merit. It was an unusual award for a small firm, especially located in the middle of the country, the Midwest.

In the process of working my company, I maintained a small export office in Munich for twenty-two years. I made many friends in Germany. However, it must be remembered that Europeans, and especially Germans would have a rather difficult time fooling someone with my experience of their past. I must admit that, throughout these years, I maintained a certain leeriness of older generation Germans. They had to clear themselves in my mind before I allowed myself to become friendly with them.

All in all, I must state without reservation that no matter where I travel the world over, there are a lot of decent people -- and a lot of thugs. It is important to distinguish between the two, and expose the latter.

Now that I am semi-retired, I am involved in community affairs, and the same principles apply here at the local level, as well as at the higher levels in the State and Federal administrations.

CHAPTER 25

COMING TO THE USA AND SUING THE GERMAN GOVERNMENT

At the end of 1945, I became engaged, and in 1946 married a local lady dentist. One of the reasons that we moved away from Bad Ischl was that I was fed up with the policies and procedures of the American Military Government. It became obvious that there would be inadequate and unsatisfactory retribution for the atrocities committed. These were political decisions made in Washington, because a new Anti-Russian, Anti-Soviet trend took place; and it was felt by the politicians that Germany would serve as a good buffer for any possible future hostilities.

I had saved a small amount of money and deposited it in the local bank in Bad Ischl. Then came the currency reform, which over night converted every old 100 Schillings into one new Schilling. My savings shrank by 99 percent, and I was virtually broke again.

Then news came from Poland that, after all the terrible happenings, and finally having a free country, the Poles again started killing the few surviving Jews. There were terrible Pogroms in 1946 in Lublin, well as in Kielce. All the displaced persons (D. P's.), and especially the survivors of the concentration camps were appalled and very angry at this news. It contributed greatly to a further polarization between the local people and the survivors, convincing many of them that their only future lay in immigrating to Israel. Many of the survivors did not want to go to Israel. They hoped to get into Canada or Australia, and above all into the United States, where they thought life would be easier. Israel was in the process of creating a new State. Conditions were very harsh and there were many hardships. It was also obvious that they would have to fight against the mighty Arab onslaught.

    My cousins in Detroit offered to take us in to begin with; so after staying for a few days in a small hotel on upper Broadway called "The Marseilles" assigned to us by the Joint Distribution Committee, we were given railway tickets and we went on to Detroit.

    Not long after I tried to determine whether any kind of restitution of our lost properties in Poland, Austria or Germany were possible. The replies were unvarying: There would be absolutely no restitution, since the properties were mostly in Poland and the Polish government would not assume any kind of responsibilities, nor would the Germans. Until today, fifty-five years after the end of the War, I am corresponding with the Austrian bank where my father worked about his pension and bank account. So far the reply is "regretfully, we can not find any documentation."

In 1982, some friends pointed out that the German Restitution Authority reopened the possibility of making certain restitution demands for a short extension period. The original term had expired long ago. When I received this notification that demands for pensions and repayments were reopened, I contacted the German Consulate in Detroit and submitted my papers. The Social Security contributions of my wages for several years working for the German construction firm were still in my possession. I made photocopies and submitted them.

The correspondence went back and forth; and the German Federal Office of Social Security denied my request.

Because of my import/export activities I maintained a small office in the city of Munich, and had become acquainted with a very nice Bavarian lawyer, Dr. Heiner Witt. On one of my visits to Munich, I showed this correspondence to Dr. Witt. He understood perfectly what transpired, and became disgusted with the bureaucratic denial of obviously justifiable rights. He explained to me that in Germany under the new Constitution you could start proceedings against the government without court costs. He offered his services free of charge because he was particularly incensed about a decision that was made on July 3, 1984 by "The Federal Insurance Office for Employees" ("Bundesversicherugnsanstalt for Angestellte"). It stated that under the documents submitted, -- " it cannot be proven that Mr. Tadeusz Chwistek was the same person as Mr. Henry Gleisner as there are serious doubts that you could change your name and have that accepted by German authorities considering that, at the time, an <u>air-tight police registration system was in operation</u>."

    This document is probably one of the reasons for writing my memoirs. It was their total indifference and contemptible obstinacy to grant credence to the conditions that prevailed in the eastern occupied territories of the Nazi empire.

    When Dr. Witt received this, he became even more dedicated to proving my rights. Several protests and petitions followed, and the answers from the German Social Security Administration always took months. Finally in February of 1987, Dr. Witt demanded, and the court agreed, that I should submit myself to a physical examination by a very famous professor. Dr. Block in Berlin, specialized in identification of persons based upon the shape of their ears. Since we had photographs of Tadeusz Chwistek on the various documents showing my right ear, I had to fly to Berlin for an appointment with Professor Dr. Block. Upon arriving I was briefly interviewed by Dr. Block, and then several photographs of my ear were taken. The professor's findings and resume were submitted immediately to the court. Believe it or not -- the Government of Germany <u>lost the case!</u> The verdict was not appealed.

On the 30th of March 1990, I finally received the first payment of my pension.

BUNDESVERSICHERUNGSANSTALT FÜR ANGESTELLTE

Versicherungsnummer: 5 9 2 3 0 3 2 4 G 0 0 8

BKZ 5065

Postanschrift:
Bundesversicherungsanstalt für Angestellte Postfach 1000 Berlin 88

Hauptverwaltung:
Berlin-Wilmersdorf, Ruhrstraße 2. Telefon (030) 865-1

Widerspruchsstelle

Mit Luftpost-Einschreiben-Rückschein

Herrn
Henry Gleisner

USA

Ihr Widerspruch vom	Durchwahl-Nr.	Datum
03.10.83 - Eingang -	(030) 865-2 18 45	-3. Juli 1984

Widerspruchsbescheid

Sehr geehrte(r) Herr Gleisner!

Die von der Vertreterversammlung der Bundesversicherungsanstalt für Angestellte (BfA) gemäß § 85 Abs. 2 Nr. 2 des Sozialgerichtsgesetzes bestimmte Widerspruchsstelle hat Ihren Widerspruch gegen den Bescheid vom _25.08.83_ geprüft und beschlossen:

Der Widerspruch wird zurückgewiesen.

Mit Ihrem Widerspruch begehren Sie die Anrechnung von Versicherungszeiten für die Zeit von Oktober 1942 bis April 1945. Sie machen geltend, unter dem Namen Tadeus Chwistek bei den Firmen A. Stronski & Co. und Wilhelm Stickel in Rawa Ruska und anderen Ostgebieten gearbeitet zu haben. Sie verweisen auf die eingereichten Arbeitsbescheinigungen.

Durch die vorliegenden Unterlagen konnte nicht bewiesen werden, daß es sich bei Tadeus Chwistek und Ihnen um ein und dieselbe Person handelt. Aufgrund des Verpflichtungsbescheides des Arbeitsamtes Berlin vom 05.03.43 ist die Einberufung zu einer OT-Einheit ab 05.08.43 auf den Namen Tadeus Chwistek erfolgt. Es bestehen Zweifel, daß Sie bei den deutschen Behörden und im Hinblick auf das damals lückenlose Meldeverfahren eine Namensänderung aufgrund falscher Papiere erreichen konnten. Es kann nicht mit hinreichender Sicherheit davon ausgegangen werden, daß Sie mit der Person des Tadeus Chwistek identisch sind, zumal Sie widersprüchliche Angaben bezüglich der Auswanderung nach Polen sowie der Annahme des falschen Namens gemacht haben. Mehrfach haben Sie angegeben, erst 1939 nach Polen ausgewandert zu sein, während in anderen Unterlagen als Zeitpunkt der Auswanderung noch das Jahr 1938 angegeben wird. Auch hinsichtlich der Annahme des falschen Namens liegen differierende Angaben zwischen den Jahren 1941 und 1942 vor. Unter Berücksichtigung der Gesamtumstände können die vorliegenden Unterlagen weder zum Nachweis noch zur Glaubhaftmachung von Beitragszeiten herangezogen werden, so daß eine Anrechnung weiterer

bitte wenden

0.5123 *
16. Aufl. - 1/84 - 50 000 - A

...e r.egulierten nicht möglich ist.

...mer Lohn- und Gehaltsklage sollte Ihrem Widerspruch der Er-
folg versagt bleiben.

Kosten des Widerspruchsverfahrens werden nicht erstattet.

PICTURE OF MY RIGHT EAR CONFIRMING MY IDENTITY TO PROFESSOR BLOCK IN BERLIN

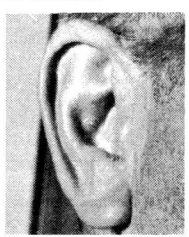

Federal insurance office for employees: "There are serious doubts that you could change your name and have it accepted by German authorities considering the air tight police registration system in effect at the time."

☐ Gegen diesen Bescheid kann innerhalb eines Monats nach Zustellung Klage beim Sozialgericht in

schriftlich oder zur Niederschrift des Urkundsbeamten der Geschäftsstelle erhoben werden. Die Frist zur Erhebung der Klage gilt auch dann als gewahrt, wenn die Klageschrift bei einer anderen inländischen Behörde oder bei einem Versicherungsträger eingegangen ist.
Die Klageschrift und nach Möglichkeit sämtliche Unterlagen sind in doppelter Ausfertigung einzureichen.

☒ Gegen diesen Bescheid kann innerhalb von drei Monaten nach Zustellung Klage beim Sozialgericht in Berlin,

Invalidenstr. 52, D-1000 Berlin 21,
schriftlich oder zur Niederschrift des Urkundsbeamten der Geschäftsstelle erhoben werden.
Die Klageschrift und nach Möglichkeit sämtliche Unterlagen sind in doppelter Ausfertigung einzureichen.

Hochachtungsvoll

gez. Paulsen   gez. Horn   gez. Vogel
Vertreter der   Vertreter der   Vertreter der
Versicherten   Arbeitgeber   Geschäftsführung

Beglaubigt
Korn
Angestellte

CHAPTER 26

OH, DU MEIN OESTERREICH!

My wife and I returned in March 1999 from an extensive trip through Europe, which included a sojourn in Austria.

"Oh, my Austria!" was the theme song of the cabaret/night-club performance of a famous Jewish-Austrian comedian before World War II. It described some of the anomalies and idiosyncrasies of Austrian life.

Austria has never come to grips in a true sense with its Nazi past. In 1943 the Moscow conference took place between Stalin, Churchill, and Roosevelt. For political reasons Austria was declared the first victim of Nazi expansion. This was done in the futile hope of driving a wedge between the Austrians and Germans. Austrian politicians had cleverly maneuvered the Allies into accepting that Austria was a victim of Nazism. They took the position that as victims they are certainly not responsible for any of the war crimes committed by the "Germans." However, the facts spoke otherwise.

According to the Vienna based Jewish Documentation Center, Austrians were accountable in some way for the death of three million Jews, about half of all those killed in the

Holocaust. A disproportionately high percentage of S.S. guards and torturers in the concentration camps were Austrian. This was quickly forgotten after the War.

Austrians fervently supported Adolph Hitler, their "native son." More than 99% of Austrians purportedly voted for the county's annexation by Germany in 1938 (The Anschluss). A well-known psychologist during an interview in Austria stated that: " Austrians seldom face up to the unpleasant aspects of their past. They have an ability to sublimate responsibility and a tendency to blame others."

Kurt Waldheim won Austria's presidency by claiming that he was a victim, first of the Nazis who ruled his country, and later of the international community, which called him to task for hiding his wartime past as a lieutenant in the German unit associated with atrocities. Many Austrian officials associated with the Hitler era held high post war government posts.

While we were in Austria, the newspapers reported the recent election in the State of Kaernten (Carinthia) of an anti-Semitic, populist, young politician, Mr. Joerg Haider. He became the head of the third largest political party in Austria, the so-called "Liberal Party" (F.P.Oe.). In the past he attacked a former Social-Democrat Prime Minister as "The Jew Kreisky". He has denied Auschwitz. He complains about the "Wiederverjudung" (renewed Jewishness) of Vienna. In 1988, as leader of a major political party, he declined to participate in the memorials of the victims of National Socialism. However, he took part in the reunions of the Waffen S. S., the very units that furnished the guards at the concentration camps. He is handsome and has good media presence, a dream picture for the Neo-Nazis.

However, his considerable wealth stems from so-called Arianization of property amassed by his S. S. father, an active Nazi party member. He acquired confiscated property that was taken away from Jewish citizens of Austria and then sold for "pennies" to deserving party members. His mother was also an active Nazi in the Hitler Jugend.

The Tri-Partite Gold Commission after the War returned the gold to Austria as it was before 1938, and Austria became one of the highest recipients per capita of Marshall Aid after the War. It is today one of the most prosperous countries in the world.

The leaders of the European Union haven't solved the contradiction between their compelling political interests in enlarging the European Union and the practical difficulties presented by their common agricultural policy, their pension plans, their unemployment benefits that are totally unrealistic. The potential costs in the future of absorbing other countries into the European Union will impose and represent a tremendous problem. Mr. Heider does not pall, but keeps reminding everyone of this uncomfortable fact. He makes relentless claims that "pristine" Austria is being "foreignized." Such appeals gave his party a 27% return of the voters in the elections of October 1999.

Austria's welfare system does not easily accommodate immigration. The overly generous social policies militate against open borders by raising suspicions among citizens that newcomers are parasites looking for generous State handouts. The argument that all an immigrant seeks is a place that will allow him to use his talents and work ethic simply gets lost when the native population hoards what the State hasn't already preempted through regulation and the claims of the tax system.

Austria and its prosperity depend primarily upon tourism and visits by foreigners to vacation in Austria. The amount of xenophobia exhibited by Heider's party will surely discourage some of the travel to Austria. Perhaps Austria needs to get hurt economically badly enough to be reminded that as a member of the European Union it can not possibly adhere to Nazi policies.

An editorial in the prestigious newspaper "Die Presse" founded in 1848, states: "Austria has an anti-Fascist constitution. Our people have voted for a responsibility to eradicate all leftovers of National Socialism. In a country such as ours, anti-fascism means also, and not least, a faith in our constitution."

That same week in March 1999 it was reported in the same newspaper that the Natural History Museum in Vienna, one of the most renowned museums in the world, "discovered" in its basement a collection of fourteen skulls of Polish partisans murdered during the Second World War. They were turned over that same week to a Polish Army delegation that came to Vienna during a ceremony, which included the Bishop of the Polish Army, the Polish Ambassador to Austria, as well as the Polish Minister of Justice.

The skulls came to Vienna in 1942 after the director of the Anthropology Department of the museum requested as many skulls of Polish people as possible from the University of Posen (Poznan) to do some "racial research." The museum paid 25 Reichsmarks a piece. They received the skulls of 15 Poles and 29 Jews. More than 6,000 victims of the Nazis had been cremated in the basement of the University of Posen and some of the skulls that were shipped to Vienna are presumably those of partisans summarily executed after capture. Similar shipments from the University were also made to the museums in Breslau, Leipzig, Koenigsberg, and Hamburg.

 A spokeswoman from the Vienna Museum stated (in 1999!) that the skeletons and skulls were never exhibited. The story is that these remains of Poles and Jews were discovered a "few years ago" during an inventory. "We had to face many sad things," said Mrs. Teschler-Nicola. "Now we are trying to clean up in some form the "ethnic derailments" (Ethnische Entgleisungen) of those times." "We hope that the skulls of the Jewish and Polish resistance fighters that we have discovered are the last remnants of the Nazi times."

 My comment is: Austria has until now NOT "cleaned up" its "ethnic derailments." This country has not been able to face its past in an honest way. One of the consequences is the ascendance of Neo-Nazi politicians into powerful political offices.

 This is just one example and reason for a kind of "love-hate" relationship with the country in which I was born -- Austria! On the one hand is the fabulous artistic and historical prominence of this country and its capital, Vienna; and on the other the shameful part of its history in this century.

After my family moved from Vienna to Warsaw, Poland, Austria was annexed by the Third Reich. The newspaper articles and photos showed an overwhelming excess of anti-Semitism, such as Hitler Youth standing over old men and women who were forced to wash the sidewalks in Vienna. My grandparents, and to a great degree also my mother were patriotic Austrians, and so I was brought up as a child in this spirit. But my numerous experiences over many years showed me a reality that was at odds with the admiration of this country of majestic beauty and history.

CHAPTER 27

FROM EXTERMINATION CAMP BELZEC TO GERMAN MILITARY CEMETERY IN ITALY

In 1972 we acquired a 14th Century gristmill the beautiful Valle dei Mulini, not far from Garda in the Province of Verona in Northern Italy.
It was in total disrepair and had no amenities. We restored it slowly over a period of years, installing water, electricity, sewage, etc. to make it a habitable vacation home. It was in the community of Costermano.
The area is outstandingly beautiful. In fact, it is probably one of the most picturesque spots in the world.
High above the Lake Garda, the German and the Italian governments established after World War II a "Soldaten Friedhof" (Soldiers Cemetery) for fallen German soldiers during World War II. Over 21,000 German officers and soldiers are buried in meticulously tended graves, each containing two fallen. The flat gravestones give rank, name, and birth and death dates.
Strangely, only one grave (as far as I could determine during my visit at the cemetery) shows

NO RANK, only the name, Christian Wirth, and the dates of birth and death.

In 1975 there was a commemoration to remember and honor the fallen German soldiers. It was organized by the Embassy of the Federal Republic of Germany. The newspapers reported that the Vice Consul from Milano declared that he would not come for the reason that, buried among the soldiers in this cemetery were some S. S. men, who were active in the extermination camps in Poland -- above all, an S. S. captain by the name of Christian Wirth. The Vice Consul must have known a lot more about Christian Wirth than I did. Shortly thereafter, the Vice Consul was fired by the foreign ministry of the Federal Republic.

Much later, I read some more about S. S. Captain Wirth.

The origin of the euthanasia killings of 1939 was an order issued by Hitler, backdated to 1 September 1939, the day of the German invasion of Poland. In this order, Hitler empowered the chief of his Chancellery, as well as his own personal physician, 'to widen the authority of individual doctors with a view to enabling them, after the most critical examination in the realm of human knowledge, to administer to incurably sick persons a mercy death. The qualifying phrases were quickly abandoned.

In Germany, the chief of the Criminal Police Office in Stuttgart, Christian Wirth, an expert in tracking down criminals -- took charge of the technical side of a more 'humane' method of killing, constructing gas chambers in which the victim was exposed to carbon monoxide gas, "a device," one SS officer later explained "which overwhelmed its victims without their apprehension and which caused them no pain."

Between January 1940 and August 1941 more than 70,000 Germans were killed by gas in 5 separate euthanasia institutions by what was called "sonderbehandlung,' 'special treatment.' The principal victims were the chronically ill, gypsies, people judged "unworthy of life" because of mental disorders, and later Soviet prisoners of war.

Subsequently, Christian Wirth's proficiency at the killing game made SS chief Heinrich Himmler appoint him to organize extermination camps in occupied Poland.

At Belzec the man in charge of the killings was Christian Wirth. It was also his task to deputize someone to organize another death camp at Sobibor. He chose a man by the name of Franz Stangl, who went to prepare the site at Sobibor. One of his helpers was Michel Hermann, who was formerly the head male nurse at the largest of the German euthanasia centers, Schloss Hartheim. Stangl, who was later convicted as a war criminal,

recalled his first visit to Belzec. "The smell," he said, "Oh, God, the smell. It was everywhere."
"Wirth was in his office. They said he was up in the camp. I asked whether I should go up -- and they said 'I wouldn't if I were you. He is mad with fury. It isn't healthy to be near him.' I asked what was the matter. The man I was talking to said that one of the pits had overflowed. They had put too many corpses in it, and putrefaction had progressed too fast, so that the liquid underneath had pushed the bodies on top up and over and the corpses had rolled down the hill. We saw some of them. Oh, God! It was awful! I said to Wirth that I couldn't do it. I simply wasn't up to the task. There wasn't any argument or discussion. Wirth just said my reply would be reported to headquarters, and I was to go back to Sobibor."
"When I got back to Sobibor, Michel and I talked and talked about it. We agreed that what they were doing was a crime. We considered deserting -- we discussed it for a long time. But how? Where could we go? What about our families?"

  Stangl continued with the construction of the gas chambers and crematoria in Sobibor. Later, he said that Wirth suddenly appeared at his camp, looked around the gas chambers on which they were still working and said, "Right! We'll try it out right now with the 25 work Jews. Get them up here." They marched our 25 work Jews up there and just pushed them in and gassed them. Michel said that Wirth behaved like a lunatic, hit out at his own staff with his whip to drive them on, and then he was livid because the doors hadn't worked properly. Wirth ordered the gas chamber doors to be changed and left.

This report was given by Franz Stangl to Gitta Sereny in Dusseldorf prison in 1971. He died the day after this last interview with her. She wrote the book: "Into that Darkness: from Mercy Killing to Mass Murder," published in London in 1974.

Stangl was an Austrian. A disproportionate percentage of Austrians served as S. S. torturers, K. Z. guards and executioners -- for reasons difficult to understand.

Christian Wirth was camp commandant at Belzec. His "guests" Dr. Wilhelm Pfannenstiel, Professor of Hygiene at the University of Marburg, and the 37-year-old chief of the Waffen SS Technical Disinfection Services, Kurt Gerstein recalled:

"We saw no dead bodies that day, but a pestilential odor hung over the whole area. Alongside the station there was a "dressing" hut with a window for "valuables. Farther on, a room designated as 'the barber'. Then a corridor 150 meters long in the open air, barbed wire on both sides, with signs: 'To the baths and inhalants.' In front of us a building like a bathhouse, to the left and right, large concrete pots of geraniums or other flowers. On the roof, the Star of David. On the building, a sign:' "Heckenholt Foundation."

The following morning, a little before seven, there was an announcement: 'The first train will arrive in ten minutes!" A few minutes later a train arrived from Lemberg: 45 cars with more than 6,000 people; 200 Ukrainians assigned to this work flung open the doors and drove the Jews out of the cars with leather whips.

A loudspeaker gave instructions: 'Strip, even artificial limbs and glasses. Hand all money and valuables in that the "valuables" window. Women and young girls are to have their hair cut in the "barber hut." (An SS Sergeant told me: 'From that they make something special for submarine crews.')

Then the march began. Barbed wire on both sides, in the rear two dozen Ukrainians with rifles. They drew near. Christian Wirth and I found ourselves in front of the death-chambers. Stark naked men, women, children and cripples passed by. A tall SS man in the corner called to the unfortunates in a loud minister's voice: 'Nothing is going to hurt you! Just breathe deep and it will strengthen your lungs. It's a way to prevent contagious diseases. It's a good disinfectant!'

They asked him what was going to happen and he answered: 'The men will have to work, build houses and streets. The women won't have to do that. They will be busy with the housework and the kitchen.

This was the last hope for some of these poor people, enough to make them march toward the death chambers without resistance. The majority knew everything; the smell betrayed it! They climbed a little wooden stair and entered the death chambers, most of them silently, pushed by those behind them.

A Jewess of about 40 with eyes like fire cursed the murderers: she disappeared into the gas chambers after being struck several times by Captain Wirth's crop. Many prayed; others asked; 'Who will give us the water before we die?'

SS men pushed the men into the chambers. 'Fill it up,' Wirth ordered. Seven to eight hundred people in 93 square meters. The doors closed. I understood the 'Heckenholt' sign. Heckenholt was the driver of the diesel whose exhaust was to kill these poor unfortunates.

Heckenholt tried to start the motor. It wouldn't start! Captain Wirth came up. You could see he was afraid because I was there to see the disaster. Yes, I saw everything and waited. My stopwatch clocked it all: 50 minutes. 70 minutes and the diesel still would not start. The people were waiting in the gas chambers. You could hear them weeping, 'as though in a synagogue,' said Professor Pfannenstiel, his eyes glued to the window in the wooden door.

Captain Wirth was furious and struck with his whip the Ukrainian who helped Heckenholt. The diesel engine started up after 2:49 by my stopwatch. 25 minutes passed. You could see through the window that many were already dead, for an electric light illuminated the interior of the room. All were dead after 32 minutes.

Jewish workers on the other side opened the wooden doors. They had been promised their lives in return for doing this horrible work, plus a small percentage of the money and valuables collected. The people were still standing like columns of stone, with no room to fall or lean. Even in death you could tell the families, all holding hands. It was difficult to separate them while emptying the room for the next batch. The bodies were tossed out, blue, wet with sweat and urine, the legs smeared with excrement and menstrual blood. Two dozen workers were busy checking mouths, which they opened with iron hooks. Dentists knocked out gold teeth, bridges and crowns with hammers.

Captain Wirth stood in the middle of them. He was in his element and, showing me a big jam box filled with teeth, said, 'See the weight of the gold! Just from yesterday and the day before! You can imagine what we find every day, dollars, diamonds, gold! You'll see!' He took me over to a jeweler who was responsible for all the valuables. They also pointed out to me one of the heads of the big Berlin store Kaufhaus des Westens, and a little man whom they forced to play the violin, the chief of the Jewish workers' commandos. 'He is a captain of the Imperial Austrian Army. Chevalier of the German Iron Cross,' Wirth told me.

Then the bodies were thrown into the big ditches near the gas chambers, about 100 by 20 by 12 meters. After a few days, the bodies swelled.

When the swelling went down again, the bodies matted down again. They told me later they poured diesel oil over the bodies and burned them in railway sleepers to make them disappear."

Christian Wirth was also very busy at Auschwitz. Dr. Kremer noted in his diary "Today I preserved fresh material from the human liver, spleen and pancreas. Also lice from persons infected with typhus in pure alcohol.

I had been for an extensive period of time interested in investigating the changes developing in the human organism as a result of starvation. At Auschwitz I mentioned this to Wirth who said that I would be able to get completely fresh material for my researches from those prisoners who were killed by phenol injections. To choose suitable specimens I visited the last block where sick prisoners from the camp came for medical examination.

During the examination the prisoners who acted as doctors presented the patients to the SS physician and described the illness. The SS physician decided then -- taking into consideration the prisoner's chances of recovery -- whether he should be treated in the hospital, perhaps as an out-patient or be liquidated.

Those attributed by the SS physician to the latter group were led away by the SS orderlies. The SS physician set aside for liquidation those prisoners whose diagnosis was 'Allgemeine Korperschwache,' 'general bodily exhaustion.'

If one of them aroused my interest owing to his advanced state of starvation, I asked the orderly to reserve the patient for me, and let me know when he would be killed by injection.

The patient was put on the dissecting table while he was still alive. I then approached the table and put several questions to the man as to such details as pertained to my researches. I asked what his weight had been before his arrest, how much weight he had lost since then, whether he took any medicines, etc.

When I had collected my information, the orderly approached the patient and killed him with an injection in the vicinity of the heart. As far as I know, only phenol injections were used. Death was instantaneous after the injection. I myself never gave any lethal injections."

Captain Christian Wirth was obviously one of the most notorious and heinous war criminals that Nazi Germany produced.

Wirth escaped from Poland when the Soviet Red Army advanced and found himself in northern Italy.

According to a report by Corriere della Sera one of the most prestigious newspapers of Italy, Wirth became the first commanding officer of the only death camp in Italy, San Sabba, located in a former rice factory in the hills above Trieste. The area around Trieste was annexed by the Third Reich in 1943, and became the capitol of the Nazi's "Adriatic administration." San Sabba was by no means a "minor" concentration camp. Anti-Fascists, Italians, Slovenians, and Jews were tortured, killed and cremated in the camp's crematorium, of which only a few stones remain today. More than 25,000 people passed through it on their way to Buchenwald, Dachau, and Auschwitz. More than 5,000 people lost their lives right there.

Later on, Himmler assigned the SS command to Odilo Globocnik, who later committed suicide to escape capital punishment for his involvement in the death of two and a half million Jews.

At the advance of the Americans into the area, Christian Wirth got into a fire fight with an American patrol and was killed. He was buried in Costermano. His grave is a desecration of this cemetery.

The Vice Consul in Milano knew the background of this story and refused to attend the commemorations services.

My beloved mother, Frieda Gleisner, was one of the victims of SS Captain Christian Wirth in Belzec.

POSTSCRIPT

In the July 2000 issue of ***"DATELINE – WORLD JEWRY*** : **"NAZI SHRINE"** – Germany is being urged to remove the remains of three Nazi war criminals buried near Lake Garda, Italy, after flowers placed at the graves raised fears that the site is becoming a shrine to right-wing extremists.

The three S.S. officers, buried alongside nearly 22,000 teenage German soldiers killed during the closing stages of the war, committed some of the worst atrocities of the period.

COSTERMANO, ITALY
GERMAN MILITARY CEMETERY
WITH 21920 FALLEN

S.S. CAPTAIN CHRISTIAN WIRTH
MASS MURDERER

WIRTH'S GRAVE – WITHOUT RANK

CHAPTER 28

FINIS

In 1962 I rented a small apartment in Munich, Germany, which I used as my European office, since I was engaged in the import and export business of sporting goods. Many people asked me how I felt living even part time among the Germans who had done so much harm to me and my family.

The explanation is not easy. I have always felt strongly about not allowing the persecutors to destroy my self-confidence. To survive, it was necessary to use a form of auto-suggestion that I was able to overcome whatever adversities or attacks I faced. My story shows how I lived, not only under the German and Soviet dictatorships, adjusted myself and did not let my spirits sag.

I could never afford to be ill. Though I were deathly sick, I had to continue to slog on. Illness was a weakness and a danger I could not afford. I had to carry on in spite of it.

During my extensive travels I met both monsters as well as many well-meaning, ethical, and decent people. I will never forget the courageous bookkeeper in Berlin, a former active member of the Social Democrat party of Germany, or the outspoken Major of the German Air Force, and many others, who risked their lives in expressing their contempt of the Nazi regime. Nor will I ever forget my dedicated friend, Dr. Heiner Witt, the Munich lawyer who battled the German government bureaucracy on my behalf.

Shortly after the War, while serving in the American Military Government in Austria, I followed the War Crimes Tribunal in Nuremberg. The condemnation and death penalty by hanging of some of the most prominent leaders of the German Nazi government had a cleansing effect upon Germany's future. The lack of this type of catharsis -- call it vengeance or retribution, if you wish -- as well as denial of the atrocities committed, is still having its devastating effects until today, the beginning of the 21st Century. Political and societal conflicts re-appear in Austria, France, and Croatia, among other places.

My personal attitude, viewpoint and resolve was and is that my presence will not be denied in any way, anywhere in the world, and particularly in Germany by the criminals of the Third Reich, or its aftermath.

I sometimes encountered uncomfortable and revolting people and situations: My next door neighbor in the Munich apartment house was an old lady in her 80's, an unreconstructed admirer of Adolph Hitler – "what wonderful autobahns he built." I explained the criminal evil of his government, but to little avail. It is difficult to debate rationally with a senile old woman. A worse case was at a horse show in Bavaria. A "riding master" from Westphalia complained about the poor behavior of his newly rich German customers. "How wonderful it was when I had the "gentlemen" from the S.S. as my riding pupils." He admired these mass murderers that in his twisted view, behaved themselves well, and paid him high fees.

By and large, my presence in Munich was comfortable and pleasant. I found that the younger generation of Germans accepted their horrible past, and wanted to overcome it as well and as fast as possible. Democracy has certainly been firmly established in the Federal Republic. The active participation in the elections; the heated, but civil debates in the Parliament; and the lively counter-demonstrations in the streets against the skinheads and Neo Nazis testify to a hopeful regeneration.

It fills me with sadness comparing this awareness with the utter absence of historical knowledge among our school children in the United States, even to the college level.

This observation is also one of the main reasons why I have written my memoirs. It is common among Holocaust survivors that they are very reluctant to revisit their nightmarish experiences.

It is important however, to set the historical record straight, and we must try to explain the unexplainable. In spite of the 1949 Universal Human Rights Declaration of the United Nations, "Ethnic Cleansing" and mass murders of innocent civilians have continued. The most effective weapon for our civilization is more and better education.

My background was not religious. The horrible persecutions, tortures and murders did not convince me about either the goodness of people in general nor about the existence of a just God. God, it can be believably argued, abandoned his "Chosen People," and many others. Perhaps a vision such as Einstein had, that there must be some kind of an overall spirit or order, is conceivably more acceptable to my thinking. Today I view the fundamentalist approach of any religion as naive at best. My abiding interest in history implanted in me so long ago by a wonderful history teacher in Vienna, tells me that religion has been, quite often, a blight on mankind. More persecution, pain, torture and death have been its result than of any other activity, theory or practice in human history. The Holocaust was one of the worst manifestations of human behavior.

Although it also had some religious roots way back, it was above all racial hatred.

I believe that as a reaction it partially pushed the State of Israel into a reality. Now after 50 plus years it influences world politics into non-acceptance of "ethnic cleansing," and mass murders. The creation of an International Court of Justice of War Crimes has finally been established.

At the same time, I cringe hearing about the "reparations," the uncovering of stolen or conveniently forgotten bank accounts in Switzerland and Austria, the disappearance of life insurance policies. All this after most survivors have died, 57 years after the events and the crimes committed.

It makes me particularly sad and angry remembering the disgraceful treatment of the concentration camp survivors in the late 1940's. How can I forget? The world was indifferent to the travails of European Jewry and others before, during and after the Holocaust.

Having said all that, and considering the Neo-Nazi movements and ultra-right politics, I must remind myself and others that in spite of all this we live in a somewhat better world. The educational work of Yad Vashem and many other organizations, and the influence of Israel have transformed humankind. We all most work toward punishing the perpetrators of the heinous crimes, the mass murderers.

The last decades have moved the world toward a greater number of democratic regimes. Let's hope we will continue in this path.

IN MEMORIAM

My mother, Frieda Gleisner, nee Than, was born in 1895 in Vienna, Austria. After my father was captured in the Lwow Ghetto and sent to the Janowska concentration camp, she remained for a while alone in the Ghetto. She wrote a postcard to me telling me she would be transported to Rawa Ruska to a "sewing job." Obviously, some German must have told her that. In effect, she perished in the gas chambers of Belzec.

My father, Jacob Gleisner, born in 1890 in Krakow, Poland (at that time part of Austria) perished in the Janowska concentration camp. After an outbreak of typhus, all prisoners were shot.

My uncle, Dr. Leon Gleisner, an attorney in Krakow, was caught by the German police in the process of creating false documents for persecuted Jews and Poles. During the interrogation in Auschwitz concentration camp, he was beaten to death.

My cousin, Zygmunt Prochaska, born in 1924 in Poland was caught with my uncle Leon. Beaten and then executed at Auschwitz.

My cousin, Janek Prochaska (John Preston), born in 1926 in Poland, was an inmate in the concentration camp of Auschwitz for four years, and survived as a hospital orderly as a Christian Pole. They conducted medical experiments on him. Before the end of the War, when the Soviets liberated Auschwitz, he joined the Free Polish Forces in Italy. He spent the rest of his life in England.

My aunt, Zofia Prochaska, nee Gleisner, born in 1888 in Krakow. She was deported to Auschwitz and never heard of again. Presumably perished in the gas chambers.

My uncle, Stefan Gleisner, also born in Krakow, Poland, was imprisoned by Soviet authorities in 1940, and spent five years in a Gulag in Kazakhstan.

****
****